D0117969

THE 7 HARDEST
THINGS GOD ASKS
A WOMAN TO DO

THE 7 HARDEST
THINGS GOD ASKS
A WOMAN TO DO

KATHIE REIMER AND LISA WHITTLE

Shepherd Press
Wapwallopen, Pennsylvania

The 7 Hardest Things God Asks a Woman to Do
©2007 by Kathie Reimer and Lisa Whittle

ISBN 978-0-9767582-5-9

All rights reserved. No part of this book may be reproduced or utilized in any form or by any means, electronic or mechanical, or by any information storage and retrieval system—except for brief quotations for the purpose of review, without written permission from the publisher. All inquiries should be addressed to: Shepherd Press, P.O. Box 24, Wapwallopen, PA 18660.

Unless otherwise indicated, all Scripture quotations are taken from the Holy Bible, New Living Translation, copyright 1996. Used by permission of Tyndale House Publishers, Inc., Wheaton, Illinois 60189. All rights reserved.
Scripture quotations marked NIV were taken from the HOLY BIBLE, NEW INTERNATIONAL VERSION®. Copyright © 1973, 1978, 1984 International Bible Society. Used by permission of Zondervan. All rights reserved.
The "NIV" and "New International Version" trademarks are registered in the United States Patent and Trademark Office by International Bible Society. Use of either trademark requires the permission of International Bible Society.
Scripture quotations marked NKJV were taken from the New King James Version. Copyright © 1982 by Thomas Nelson, Inc. Used by permission. All rights reserved.
Scripture quotations marked NASB were taken from the NEW AMERICAN STANDARD BIBLE®, Copyright © 1960, 1962, 1963, 1968, 1971, 1972, 1973, 1975, 1977, 1995 by The Lockman Foundation. Used by permission.

Italics or bold text within Scripture quotations indicate emphasis added.

Page design and typesetting by Lakeside Design Plus
Cover design by Tobias' Outerwear for Books

Printed in the United States of America

Contents

Acknowledgments

Kathie's Thanks

With a heart completely filled with love and gratitude for our precious family team, God's indescribable gifts to me:

To Jim, my faithful love

To Mark, Nichole, Lukas, and Cade

To Lisa (What a privilege to write this book with you! You're my precious friend.) Scotty, Graham, Micah, and Shae.

To Jenifer, Nathan, and Baby-we-love.

All of you are my daily encouragers, my unconditional cheering section—and my every-waking-moment *joy*! Thank you for letting me use so many of your stories in the book.

Lisa's Thanks

Heavenly Father, I am your work in progress. Thank you, far above all others, for creating me to be the person I am . . . and for helping me finally realize who that is.

To Scotty, my wonderful husband—thank you for taking over many of the bath, bedtime, and carpool duties while I was writing this book, and for giving up time with me in the process. Most of all, thank you for letting me be me. I love you so much!

Graham, Micah, and Shae Elisabeth, my beautiful children—The three most "awesome creations" I have ever been given. You are my dreams, my joy, and my life.

Dad— You have always been and will always be my "bigger than life" hero.

Mark and Jen—you are two of my favorite people in the world. It's cool that we're related!

To Mom, the "birth mother" of this project, and coincidentally, me—thank you for the privilege of letting me share this book with you. It is an honor to be included in any capacity with you. You are it: the mom, the wife, the MiMi, the woman. You are all I strive to be.

A Special Thanks from Both of Us

To the seventy-one women at our home church of Hickory Grove Baptist, North Campus, in Charlotte, N.C., who allowed themselves to be our "test group" for this material. Your faithfulness to the class and to the Lord, inspired us to make this manuscript available to others.

Thanks, Brenda McDowell, for your encouragement and support that helped make it happen. We love you!

Preface

It's funny how things "happen."

About seven years ago, my mother and I were sitting on the floor of her Atlanta home, playing with my then one-year-old son. Over the squeaks and rattles of my son's toys, we talked about our desire to write a book together. We looked for ways to connect the necessary dots to do so. We brainstormed over topics and discussed philosophies for nearly an hour. Frustrated over how it was not coming together, we jotted down a few notes and closed the notebook. We never picked it back up again.

Fast forward five years. My mother called to tell me about a book idea she had. She was going to submit a proposal for *The Hardest Things God Asks a Woman to Do* to a few publishing houses to see if anyone would be interested. With three books under her belt, she already had relationships with some publishers. When she told me what the book would be about, it immediately struck a chord. Actually it was more like a lightning bolt. Looking back I know God was trying to tell me something but I was unaware of it at the time. I told Mom it was a super idea and I would pray about the future of it, if there were to be one.

Some months later, my mother informed me that the proposal had been rejected. She looked at it as a closed door and a closed issue. I told her I loved the idea and thought the information in it would be helpful to women, but that is the only thought I had about it that day.

Soon afterwards, my church's women's ministry director, a good friend, asked me if I would be interested in teaching an eight-week Bible study on Wednesday nights. I hesitated; I had no prepared material. Suddenly, a name and an idea popped into my head: *The hardest things God asks a woman to do.* Since my mother and I had taught together in the past, I knew this would be a great opportunity to do something together again. After some cajoling and convincing, my gracious mother agreed to do the class with me.

We laugh now at our naivety in saying yes. At that time we had no content, only titles and ideas. We jotted down the top seven hardest things, with the intent to teach seven classes and leave room for one extra session, should we need one. With only a couple of months to go before the study started, my busy teacher-mother and this mom of three young children set out to write something worthy of a woman's time in the midst of a chaotic week. It was a wonderful yet daunting task.

The class began with seventy-one women. Each week my mother and I took turns discussing "hardest things," feeling amazed at how it had all come together. Admittedly, we both were nervous on the weeks that did not belong to us, trusting that the other would show up with something to say. And by the awesome grace of God, he showed up—and taught through us. God had been the One doing the planning all along.

At the end, we breathed a huge collective sigh of relief and praised God for the incredible blessing we had received from the privilege of sharing our thoughts with others. Long-winded as we both are, we uncovered another blessing: we had enough material for a book on the subject. Hence, this book was born.

As a mother and daughter functioning as a team, our passion for this book comes from our deep desire to see women realize the liberating truths written in God's Word about some of the hardest things God asks a woman to do. While these "hardest things" appear to be in contradiction to each other, they are both applicable and integral to our lives as Christian women. They coincide while remaining essentially independent of one another. Our hope and prayer is that by identifying them and dealing with them in a straightforward manner, we will come to a better understanding of the freedom that comes with knowing what is required of us—and the empowerment of the Lord who guides, strengthens, and enables us to do what he asks.

On a personal note, one of the greatest blessings in writing this book was the fantastic privilege of doing it together. When people ask me about how the book evolved, I tell them that my mother was its birth mother and I was its adoptive mother. It's no real wonder that our planning session on my mother's floor seven years ago didn't work out; I believe it is because this project was not yet ready to be born. I see a great deal of irony in that fact, and I believe it was his plan all along for us to write this book together.

While you may notice some distinct differences in our writing style and content, you need to know that the differences don't stop there. We are two different women with very different personalities; this allows us to cover issues from different seasons of life and varying temperament-types that are universal to all Christian women.

That's really what this book is all about. It doesn't matter what your age is, what your socioeconomic status is, how many children you do or don't have, or where you are in your Christian walk. The hardest things God asks a woman to do are hard for everyone, everywhere, everyday. But in the end they are the most rewarding and fulfilling.

Thank you for the honor and joy of sharing them with you.

— Lisa Whittle
Charlotte, N.C.,
September 2006

Single-Focus/Multi-Task

Kathie

uite often my husband of nearly forty years and I have some version of the following conversation, sometimes gently spoken, but usually with a bit, or a lot, of emotion in our voices. The conversation invariably occurs when we have a limited amount of time and several things to get done.

For instance, I suggest something like this as we're parking the car at the strip mall: "Honey, why don't you go to the bank next door while I run in and mail this and make a copy of this—and we'll meet back here at the grocery store in ten minutes."

Sounds like a perfectly good plan to me. But he says, "No, dear. Let's do one thing at a time. You come with me to the bank and then I'll go with you to the post office and the store."

My husband is a single-focus man, and I'm a multi-tasking woman. After all these years we should know that and function accordingly.

But our dilemma is, basically, irresolvable. It can't be fixed, unless I single-focus *with* him, while my internal multi-tasking engine idles at full speed and I'm thinking, *We could get this all done so much faster and more efficiently.*

Single-Focus Versus Multi-Tasking

While single-focusing is a very good thing, for most women (and some men) multi-tasking is the only real option we live with.

Like a juggler, we bounce a baby, or grandbaby on one hip while mixing cookie ingredients as we stir the Hamburger Helper on the stove, with a cell phone tucked under our ear just as the UPS man knocks at the door, right before having to scold the preschooler at our side for interrupting yet again and tattling on his brother who allegedly called him a really bad name like "fuzzyhead." All during a five-minute interval in a fairly unstressed ordinary day.

Women who work outside the home face similar challenges. The boss says, "Get this report on my desk in three minutes," and plops it on top of the assignments already impatiently calling your name. Meanwhile, perpetual in-coming calls must be instantaneously ana-lyzed and routed just as the computer dies and your co-worker in the next cubicle calls out in a depressed voice, "Are you busy right now?"—right before the babysitter phones to report that the baby won't stop crying and your kindergartener's school says he is sick and must be picked up *right away.*

When do women *ever* get to single-focus? Never. Never, ever, ever. Multi-tasking is a way of daily life for us. Doing only one thing at a time is a luxury saved for birthdays or anniversaries when some kind-hearted somebody allows you a long, luxurious bath without a child playing in the bathroom beside you, dumping non-water-resistant objects into your bath or knocking wildly at the door, crying, "Can I come in, Mommy?"

Nevertheless, in its always relevant and truthful way, the Bible talks about the value of having a single focus *and* being able to spiritually multi-task at the same time. The way my husband operates isn't the only right way. But neither is mine. We *both* must do *both*.

Remember those 3D posters of dots and tiny shapes and colors that were trendy for a while? They were called Magic Eye stereogram pictures and they started showing up in the early 1990s everywhere, in storefront windows and at swap meets. To see a pattern you were supposed to focus at the center and not look away for a second. A little crowd would gather, with people making comments like, "I don't see anything, do you?" I've done it myself, feeling a little silly, since I couldn't see anything but a bunch of dots, but I felt a need to act as if I could.

Finally, after several long minutes of single-focusing, someone would triumphantly shout, "I see it! Look. There's the face of Elvis." Or George Washington, or the Statue of Liberty, or whatever had magically appeared. The rest of us would give up, or maybe smile and nod, mortified by the fact that we seemed to be the only person in the world who never saw a single picture from among the multitude of dots.

What does God say about our single-focus? Should we have just one? What should it be? You mean my husband was right, after all?

God Calls Women to Focus

It turns out that the Bible emphasizes over and over again the need to have a single focus.

A single focus in our faith. "There is one body and one Spirit—just as you were called to one hope when you were called—one Lord, one faith, one baptism; one God and Father of all, who is over all and through all and in all" (Ephesians 4:4–6 NIV).

15

A single focus in our convictions. "One thing I do know. I was blind but now I see." (John 9:25 NIV).

A single focus in our mind-set, thoughts, and choices. "He who doubts is like a wave of the sea, blown and tossed by the wind...He is a double-minded man, unstable in all he does" (James 1:6, 8).

A single focus in our actions. "But one thing I do: Forgetting what is behind and straining toward what is ahead, I press on toward the goal to win the prize for which God has called me heavenward in Christ Jesus" (Philippians 3:13–14 NIV).

As believers, we'll never be politically correct. We'll never be able to say that Allah or Buddha or whatever other god is worshiped is as true as the triune God of the Bible. Our single focus can only be on Jesus, because he alone deserves to be the focal point for everything we *are*, all that we *do*, and our single driving motivation behind it all, everyday. As he said, "I am *the* Way, *the* Truth, *the* Life—no one comes to the Father but by me" (John 14:6). The old hymn says: "Turn your eyes upon Jesus / Look full in His wonderful face / and the things of earth will grow strangely dim / in the light of His glory and grace." It's true. Psalm 16:5 tells us, "Lord, you *alone* are my inheritance, my cup of blessing."

Focusing on Jesus Amid Chaos

Focal points in life are important. When we drive at night facing oncoming traffic in the opposite lane, it is important not to look directly at the lights coming our way, but to focus on our own lane. A juggler has to have a point of focus that allows him not to be distracted by the flurry of balls going around. While experiencing the intensity of childbirth, a mother is encouraged to focus on one spot in the room to endure all that is happening around and within her.

For the Christian, the most critical, foundational thing that God asks us to do or to focus on, is Jesus Christ. At the same time, he knows that the assignment will be hard. The call of the immediate, the urgent, the necessary, and the unexpected will constantly resound in our ears and grab at our attention. We won't find it possible to mute life's raucous clamor—or to change the dial on "reality radio" to a more environmentally-soothing station. Our single focus on Jesus Christ must exist amid the chaos of life.

The requirement that our central focus be on Jesus Christ accompanies an elemental truth regarding fallen human nature. God knows that unless Jesus is our number one focus, we invariably will be focused on *our* life, *our* family, *our* ideas, *our* plans, *our* needs, *our* wants, and *our* resulting frustration because all of life's loose ends will just keep on flapping. Peace, joy and fulfillment will continue to elude us. Without a central focus on Jesus, all of our well-meaning spiritual multi-tasking will only amount to a random frenzy of pointless, misdirected energy and activity. As we frantically try to "juggle" life's demands, some going this way, others going that way, going up, coming down, at times eluding our grasp, we will inevitably be left spiritually and physically exhausted. While trying to gather all that we've dropped, we wonder, *If this is God's plan for a productive spiritual life, I'd trade it all for one day of peace and joy and some plain old R & R.*

If Jesus is just one of our many points of focus, compartmentalized and relegated to the "religious" side of our lives, but not at the center of it, our life will be much like trying to look into a kaleidoscope with both eyes open. We won't be able to focus well. Life's color wheel will appear as a bunch of random shapes and colors, and we'll constantly be distracted by everything going on around us because of double vision. Only as we focus on Jesus, will all of life come together into a picture of unity, beauty, and purpose.

Focusing Our Affections on Jesus

When I was a little girl, we had something very antiquated called "records." When a record was placed on the little post that was designed to fit in the hole in the middle of the record, the record would spin around and around smoothly, like a big, black CD. But if the record were put on the player just a little off center, it wobbled, shook and played distorted music—like a CD that's off track. The same is true in our lives when Jesus isn't our central, single focus. So how do we fix that?

Colossians 3:2 (KJV) says, "Set your affection on things above, not on things on the earth" [meaning to fall deeply in love with Jesus, and things of eternal value]. We have the ability and the responsibility to set our affection and attention on Jesus, on what really matters, and what will last forever and ever.

God asks a woman to do something hard, not impossible. He never asks the impossible—never, ever—because he provides the "can do" part of the assignment and promises to make sure all expectations are met.

Refocusing on Jesus

However, even after we have set our minds on eternally valuable things, we may have to refocus often, to frequently spray spiritual window cleaner on the lens of our heart to keep a clear focus. We may have to press the reset button of our mind many times during the day as life pulls, shouts, and clamors for our attention, and our focus becomes blurry and distorted.

A friend of mine, a young mother named Hilary, moved with her husband and baby girl into a beautiful new house near a lake. As Hilary worked at planting flowers around the front of their home, she often noticed a duck "couple" waddling through her yard. One day the spectacular drake and his rather plain "wife" selected the bush beside her front stairway as their spot-of-choice to take up housekeeping. The next day Hilary saw that an impressive nest had been constructed. The female duck was now perched upon it, seemingly oblivious to everything around her.

A yard crew came. They cut, edged, and blew with their ominous-looking equipment, inches away from the momma-to-be. Delivery men came and went, neighborhood children ran squealing through the yard every afternoon, car brakes screeched on the nearby street, the family dog barked and lunged at the sitting duck time and time again. Nothing rattled Mrs. Duck's resolve.

Without a glitch in her concentration, a fluff of a feather, or the slightest indication of apprehension, the mother duck remained immovable on the nest, focused totally on her task-at-hand, producing ducklings. Fuzzy, quacking babies. At the appointed time, out popped the fruit of her labor, and mother and ducklings headed for the lake. (By the way, where was dad all this time?)

We need to constantly remind ourselves to refocus intently on Jesus as we move through daily life. Maybe for you that would mean posting an artist's rendering of His kind eyes in a strategic spot, or turning off your car radio and experiencing some solitude. Maybe it would help to place a Scripture verse, or just the word *focus* on your refrigerator, or leave your Bible open on the kitchen counter to a place that God's Spirit has made meaningful for you.

I became convicted recently that I was a news junky. I was too often checking to see if anything new was happening on the news channel and filling too much of my day with meaningless chatter and unnecessary background noise. I became aware that even informative, educational "lures" had the tendency to move my focus away from Jesus' presence in my life. I began to wonder how loudly Jesus had been shouting to my heart, just to try to carry on a conversation with me. I had been as deaf to his still, soft voice as I would have been if my spiritual hearing had been damaged by auditory overload.

My wonderful mother lived with us for the last five years of her life. During one of the last trips we took running errands around town, we passed through the industrial district of the city, replete with factories, car graveyards, and deserted storefronts. Mother and

I hadn't spoken for several minutes when she broke the silence with the excited exclamation, "Oh, just look at that *beautiful* tree."

Outside her window I saw only a junkyard full of rusty metal objects and discarded trash. Then, to my amazement, I saw the tree. The fall foliage that adorned it was truly breathtaking. But even more awe-inspiring to me, even now as I think of it, was the knowledge that my dear mother had the blessed ability to see past all the junk to the beauty beyond. That one sentence expressed the heart of who she was and always had been: a lovely lady who lived each day in the constant awareness of the Lord's presence and his magnificent handiwork all around her.

Sometimes we need to focus on Jesus because of the stormy, threatening, frightening times we face. At other times we need our eyes to be fixed on the beauty of Jesus because of all the debris in our lives, all the junk, all the "stuff" that commands our attention.

He Is Focused on Us

We need to remember that even when *we* don't focus on Jesus, he is always, constantly focused on us. Consider Psalm 16:7–9: "I will bless the Lord who guides me. Even at night my heart instructs me. I know the Lord is always with me. I will not be shaken, for he is right beside me. No wonder my heart is filled with joy."

I grew up in a suburb of Los Angeles, where my family lived in a large apartment complex near my father's work and the kindergarten class I attended. In those "gentler and kinder" times, I walked the couple of blocks to school in the morning and back home each afternoon by myself. My parents instructed me not to talk to strangers, but since abductions of children were not commonplace, I usually felt safe. However, it was the time of the Cold War, and since an enemy attack was regarded as a possibility, every week a warning siren would sound so that families could practice what they would do if such a scenario should actually occur.

One day on my walk home, the ominous scream of the air-raid siren suddenly split the silence around me and fear gripped my heart. I ran into a nearby stairwell and assumed the prescribed position: crouched, face-down, hands-covering-head as I had been instructed to do in case of an actual attack. Almost instantly, I heard my mother's sweet voice, reassuring me, coming quickly closer and closer until I felt her arms around me, lifting me up to hold me close.

As calm replaced fear, I asked how she had known where I was, since I always made my homeward trek alone and thought I was completely hidden from sight. She said, "Honey, I always watch you all the way home from the time you leave the school. And Jesus is with you—you're *never* alone." Jesus, our loving heavenly parent, is always there for us. In Isaiah 43:4 the Lord assures us, "You are precious to me. You are honored, and I love you."

The popular Christian music group Caedmon's Call inspires us with these incredible words of truth from their 2002 song, "Before There Was Time":

> Before there was time
> You counted the hairs on my head
> You knew all the words that I've said
> And You purchased me back from the dead
> Before I was made
> You searched me and knew my ways
> You numbered all my days
> And You set forth the steps I would take[1]

If Jesus focuses on us with such love, how can we ignore his gaze and carelessly look away to all the trivial distractions around us? Remember the words of the classic hymn, "Turn Your Eyes Upon Jesus":

> O Soul, are you weary and troubled?
> No light in the darkness you see?
> There's light for a look at the Savior
> And life more abundant and free.

So, turn your eyes upon Jesus.
Look full in His wonderful face,
And the things of earth will grow strangely dim
In the light of His glory and grace. [2]

God Asks Women to Multi-Task

When we think of multi-tasking, we might say to ourselves, "Oh, I know what that is. I'm an experienced multi-tasker. I do it in my sleep!"

Even our bodies are multi-taskers. Just think about all the amazing jobs your physical body is doing right this minute: breathing, heart beating, blood flowing, cells multiplying, eyes blinking, tears forming, tonight's dinner turning into fat (straight from our mouth to our thighs), our mind going a hundred miles an hour. We are multi-tasking machines every single minute we live.

If you're a mom or grandmom of little children, have you noticed how many cartoon characters have more than two arms or legs so they can get more done with more power? Sometimes they are the good guys like Inspector Gadget (who has extra handy-dandy arms and gadgets in his hat and shoes) or Doc Ock in Spiderman, (the bad guy with four sinister arms). It would be helpful at times to actually have more arms, more hands, more than just a left and right side to our brain so we could get more done, more efficiently, in less time.

When we think of spiritual multi-tasking, we tend to extend our perception to "doing" things for God, volunteering at our church, saying, "Sure, I'll do it" every time a need is mentioned. Every spare minute is filled with serving on multiple committees, engaging in projects for non-profit causes, and on and on, until, honestly, our tongue is hanging out, our heartbeat has become irregular, our blood-pressure's sky-high, and we're snapping at everybody, like an alligator in jeans, a gray sweat shirt and a baseball cap.

Why do we let ourselves get into that pitiable, wiped-out condition? Most of the time we spiritually multi-task because we love God, and we want, some day, to present him with a long list of good things we did for him. We think that if more squares on our calendar are filled with spiritual activities, and our name appears on the list of people involved in organizing church events, the happier he is with us and the closer we are to becoming highly regarded "spiritual giants."

And, then, to make matters worse, if we're not careful, we do all those good things *in our own strength*, which is completely energy-depleting and unfulfilling. Besides that, all our efforts will one day burn up, because "without him we can do nothing."

We look in the mirror at a burned-out, empty-hearted lady when we had hoped that our reflection would be one of the Holy Spirit living through us. Multi-tasking is hard, especially when we do it the wrong way.

The Bible describes many wonderful people who were busy doing things in the name of Jesus and for his glory: Martha, the disciples passing out food, believers ministering to the sick, the poor and the widows. We are to be *his* hands and feet with human hearts. We are the "pipeline" through which he can bless others.

But, as important as being involved in service for him truly is, God's multi-tasking "to do" list is much more about who we *are* than what we *do*.

Our spiritual multi-tasking list is really a "to be" list.

We could take that list from almost anywhere in the Bible. We could be the wonder woman in Proverbs 31. We could be the armor-clad spiritual warrior in Ephesians. We could be the lady looking in a mirror and seeing herself for who she really is in the book of James. We could be the person in Matthew 7, juggling spiritual balls and remembering not to worry, not to judge, to be sure to keep on praying, to do good things for others, to beware of false teachers, to be genuine, to produce good spiritual fruit. We could be glad for trouble,

23

as we ask for wisdom—as we are patient, as we are quick to listen, slow to speak, slow to get mad—as we avoid evil, obey God, control our tongue, and give to orphans and widows. We could choose any important list we want from the Bible, and all those things are spiritual characteristics that we are to demonstrate simultaneously every day. Whoever said that believers are weak people?

So, let's look at some key "multi-tasks," some examples of spiritual doing and being that Jesus will perform in and through us, as we let him. They are part of the package Jesus promised when he said, "I am come that they might have life, and that they may have *it* more abundantly" or "My purpose is to give life in all its fullness" (John 10:10 NKJV and NLT).

The divinely practical principles that lead to all the abundance God has promised—the tasks that Jesus asks us to perform because of who he enables us to be—may be very familiar. But, remember, they may be hard.

We've already seen that God wants us to be focused people. He also has some additional things in mind for us to do and be—some spiritual "balls" to juggle for his glory and for our great benefit.

First: Be Grateful

God asks us to be grateful. In 1 Thessalonians 5:18, the apostle Paul says, "in everything give thanks; for this is God's will for you in Christ Jesus" (NASB). We might as well start with the tough task of dissecting this verse. The first word God gives us in this Scripture is the little, innocent-sounding word, *in.* No big deal, just *in.* But this *in* means right in the middle of situations that we face, good and bad—not when they're over, not after they have played out to the finish, not after we've seen why they happened, not after we've avoided them, but *in* them.

Here's an even bigger whammy. *Everything.* Everything? Bad things, accidents, sickness, death, messes, unfulfilled expectations, entanglements that somebody's sin has caused? In the middle of those things? Give what? Thanks? Yes. Why? How? James says, "Dear brothers and sisters, whenever trouble comes your way, let it be an opportunity for joy." Think of trouble as a blessing. Wow! That is hard.

I have two wonderful friends, Mary and Becky. They will probably never meet until they recognize each other in heaven, but they have traveled similar earthly paths. Both have had an immeasurable impact upon my life and the lives of many others. Both are God's precious "angels" and his special personal "gifts" to me. Though they live miles apart, their lives are parallel in many aspects. Both ladies have faced unbelievable betrayal by the men they had every reason to believe would be godly, loving husbands. The false face of each man was eventually removed through events out of his wife's control. When they were, the corruption and hypocrisy, the double-lives, were vividly and excruciatingly revealed.

The real lives of Becky and Mary and their families include years of coping with abuse in a myriad of ways. On one terrible occasion, Mary's husband picked her up and threw her against the wall, fracturing her hip and shattering her spirit into a thousand tiny pieces. For years, Becky's beautiful life was just as deeply wounded and splintered because of indescribable addictions in her husband's life and it seemed as if she would never again experience peace and joy.

These two beautiful women suffered the pain of infidelity over and over. Even well-meaning friends did not always understand their terrible plight and as a result, unknowingly, inflicted greater pain upon them.

Compounding their hurt was the pain dealt to their children. Both Mary and Becky were two-in-a-million moms in their selfless devotion to their children, for whom they made every imaginable maternal sacrifice to provide a stable home in a completely volatile situation. They provided music lessons, opportunities to play on sports teams, and other advantages for their children that required their own personal sacrifice. (Many of you know—you're there right now.)

The list of tragedies goes on and on . . . serious illness, loneliness, tremendous loss. Again and again these precious ladies have pondered the dreams they had as starry-eyed brides; visions of a loving marriage and happy, blessed children, enjoying the life that God designed. But, in every situation, each lady has a simple statement that expresses the beauty and sincerity of her heart. She simply smiles her lovely smile and says, quietly, "God is good." Because he is.

"In everything give thanks, for this is the will of God in Christ Jesus." Was it the will of God for the husbands of Mary and Becky to injure and abandon them? Was the abuse inflicted upon them and their children God's will? Did he want two committed believers to have to struggle and raise their children alone? Those things were the will of God? God's will was for them to grow to be like Christ, to shine like stars, to give him glory, and to *give thanks* even in the middle of all of it. And they did.

Some of you can top these stories. Many of us have faced things that make absolutely no sense to us, no matter how much we search the Scriptures and try to discern the mind of God. We have experienced events so excruciatingly difficult in our lives that what we faced still seems to have no reason, no redeeming quality, no purpose at all. And some of you are agonizingly there right now.

Some of the most difficult circumstances we experience are not just those that seem unfair and unnecessary. Equally hard to endure are all those situations and entanglements that we have had a part in creating for ourselves and others. We've done something foolish, irresponsible, unethical, immoral, or impulsive, and now we must face the ramifications of our own choices and behavior, and watch the effect those mistakes and sins have had on the people we care about most.

As beloved children, we experience the eternal Father's sheltering, comforting, healing presence throughout our lives, but we don't exist in a trouble-free bubble of ease. This is earth, not heaven.

Matthew Henry was a well-known and loved Bible commentator. One day he was robbed and later wrote about this experience in his personal diary. His journal entry revealed an important key to our being able to give thanks in everything. These were his words:

> Let me be thankful—
> First, because I was never robbed before.
> Second, because although they took my wallet, they did not take my life.
> Third, because although they took my all, it was not much.
> And fourth, because it was I who was robbed, not I who robbed.

Incredibly, God asks us to give him thanks right in the middle of all kinds of bad circumstances, and that's not easy for us. But, we can remember and remind ourselves until it penetrates to the very heart of who we are, and how we think and act, that God is always good and always with us, and he will bring good and beauty from the ashes all around us. He is always gracious, always strong, always able, always faithful, always loving—and always present.

In 2 Corinthians 2:14, God promises that we will always triumph in Christ Jesus. As believers, when we're in the middle of things, we're in Christ Jesus. For that awesome truth we can always be grateful.

Second: Be Content

The second hard task God asks of us is to be content. Paul is very specific about this topic. He says "Godliness with contentment is great gain" (1 Timothy 6:6 NKJV) and "Do everything without complaining or arguing," (Philippians 2:14 NIV). Contentment walks hand-in-hand with gratitude. The existence of both attributes depends on our single focus, our perspective, our priority, our perception of what is really important.

It's natural for us to ask a lot of God; we need him, we depend on him to take care of us, we cry to him when we get in a jam. We don't hesitate for a minute to ask for really big things of him. Everything changes, however, when we think that God is asking a lot of us. We start to murmur and complain. Murmuring and complaining often show up as a dark attitude that we feed and pamper and carry around in our pocket all day. Discontentment appears as "dirty looks" we aim like daggers, a cold shoulder, or an icy response. Even if we don't verbalize our complaints, we mull over them and become self-absorbed when we could be living life abundantly.

What do we complain about in the middle of everyday life's multi-tasking? You probably can add to my inventory: Picking up our husband's or kid's clothes, a husband who's away a lot or works late, muddy tracks on a clean floor or carpet, whining, temper tantrums, sibling warfare, interrupted sleep, an annoying coworker, a hard-to-tolerate mother-in-law, a difficult teenager, something we don't like about ourselves, our financial situation.

There is a funny little children's book entitled *It Could Be Worse*. In this story, on each new page, things do go from bad to worse. In our "real lives," it's not a bad idea to think about how our situation could really be worse than it is—because it always could be.

It may sound a little silly, but we can help raise our contentment level by voicing simple counter-thoughts to our complaints. Here are examples:

"Yes, I got a ticket, but I didn't have an accident."

"Yes, I have arthritis, but I'm not bound to a wheelchair."

"Yes, my son has trouble being kind and obedient, but he's good at math."

"Yes, my daughter may never be called pretty, but she loves God and has a heart for people."

"Yes, I'm single, but I have many wonderful friends."

"Yes, my husband doesn't know Christ, but he's not hostile to Christianity."

"Yes, my house is old and small, but it's warm and secure and paid for."

It all goes back to our focus. If God alone is our focus, it won't make much difference in the long or short run if our dear husband never picks up his clothes. After all, he works so we can buy clothes. Gratitude and contentment are linked.

Dr. Viktor Frankl was a Jewish psychiatrist who spent three horrific years in Auschwitz concentration camp. Because of his interest in the emotional and physical well-being of people, he noticed the responses of his fellow prisoners to their dehumanizing experiences. Dr. Frankl noticed that some strong men in the camp quickly gave up hope and died while others, who physically appeared much weaker, survived.

As he reported his observations later, Dr. Frankl recalled being intrigued by a few men who sacrificed their last rations of food to give what little they had to someone else whose need they perceived was worse than their own. Those individuals demonstrated, according to Dr. Frankl, that the one last human freedom that remains available to a man, after everything else has been stripped from him, is his ability to choose the way he will react to his circumstances.

The Bible reveals the same profound truth. We can, and God asks us to, *choose* to give thanks, to be grateful in all circumstances of life. (We decide, he enables.)

In my hurry to get to work one early morning, my otherwise-preoccupied mind was not focused on the eventualities on the road ahead, and in a split second of time, a squealing of tires and the tremendous pop of an airbag, I found myself as the perpetrator of a rush hour fender bender. "Yes, officer, it was my fault."

After facing the embarrassment of curious eyes, the clanking and screeching of dented and dangling fenders as I endeavored to move my wounded vehicle out of the traffic flow to the shoulder of the road, I began to make the necessary arrangements to get on with my day and repair the damage my carelessness had caused.

As I made contact with the various members of my family, not one asked of me, "How much damage did you do to the car?" Each precious one queried with obvious concern, "Are you okay, honey?" "Are you all right, Mom?"

We can let the first ball that we're juggling, being grateful, also help us to learn to be content. Not to say we never should make changes in bad situations when we can, but, honestly, practically-speaking, how can we look at pants, socks, and underwear on the floor and be truly content? We can be grateful we have a husband that comes home to us at night. What about a husband who has to work late? He's working, and there are others things he could be doing late at night that he's not. What about dirty diapers and mountains of laundry? Lots of women would give everything they own to have a baby.

To be content, we can't forget what really matters: the Lord himself, the people he's allowed to be in our lives, and the people he allows our lives to touch.

Third: Be Mindful

There is a third multi-tasking principle on our spiritual "to be" list that God asks of us, which makes it much easier for us to be grateful and to be content. It's a subtle one: Be mindful.

Our mindset, the way we think, affects how we *look* at life's circumstances, other people, even ourselves and it determines what we *do* after we are done thinking. Proverbs 23:7 (KJV) tells us, "As a man thinketh in his heart, so is he." Or, to paraphrase it, the way a woman thinks, determines who she *is*, and eventually impacts what she *does*.

How many days do we spend most of our "thinking" time focused on someone or something we're upset with, usually our husband or our boss or a coworker, and often we then *act* based on those thoughts.

One morning our husband makes an innocent comment about our hair, our size, or something we did, and we begin to think about what he said. We think about it all day, getting madder and more defensive, until we've built an oversize case on our own behalf that we could take to court. In the evening he asks, "How was your day, honey?" We give him the look and say, "Like you really care." He has no clue what we're talking about or what in the world set us off. So what are we supposed to think about? Check out Philippians 4:8:

> Finally, brethren, whatever things are true, whatever things are noble, whatever things are just, whatever things are pure, whatever things are lovely, whatever things are of good report, if there is any virtue and if there is anything praiseworthy—meditate on these things" (NKJV).

Let's take a look at a few of these good things.

God asks us to think about things that are true. Some information we spend precious time thinking about, that has been passed on to us in the form of "news" about someone else, may not even be true. If we're not sure, whatever the information is, it probably doesn't deserve to occupy our thoughts. Whatever things are true—think about *those* things.

God asks us to think about pure things. As you know, it's not just men who have impure, lustful thoughts; women do too, especially if those thoughts have romantic components and romance is missing from their lives. Women, too, have affairs; an affair usually involves a man *and a woman*. According to recent statistics, infidelity among married women is just as great as infidelity among married men.

In a family at church, the wife began to conduct an internet affair in a chat room. What began as a random connection blossomed from a casual conversation into a full-bloom emotional affair. Although the two participants never physically met, their email relationship was just as real and damaging to their marriage relationships as it would have been if they had actually met in person.

Remember, too, that temptation by itself is not sin; Jesus was tempted just as we are and he was sinless, but it's important to control what happens next. How much do we dwell on that temptation or think about that spark of chemistry we feel about somebody that's not our husband? My little grandmother often quoted the wise adage that describes our human experience, "You can't keep the birds from flying over your head, but you can keep them from building a nest in your hair." Temptation is inevitable; yielding to its enticement is optional.

I believe Satan takes those lustful thoughts and entices us by enhancing them and making them bigger and bigger until they are literally more exciting, more alluring than real life. Many times, when the offenders finally come to their senses, they are absolutely devastated with what they have done to themselves, their children, their spouses, to another family, their testimonies, their future, their Lord.

But, thanks be to God who is a God of grace and forgiveness for all sin; he has restored many who have been down the path of impurity in their lives. We always need to remember that we're all vulnerable to the same sins that others have committed—and even if we don't fall prey to their enticement, the Bible says that if we have broken any commandment, we're guilty of them all. Whatever things are pure, think on these things.

God says to think about things of good report. So many things fall into this category: good news, enlightenment from his Word, wonderful things people do for others, kind words that have been said, positive plans, projects, and activities, things to look forward to, hugs and affirmation from those we love and value, progress in areas we're trying to improve, and smiles and words of encouragement we've received and want to pass on to someone else. The list goes on and on.

We're not being unrealistic Pollyannas to fill our minds with thoughts of "good report." As believers in Jesus Christ we're constantly surrounded without and within with wonderful, positive information that deserves our attention and deserves to be passed on. The flip side to thinking about good reports is thinking about bad reports. Lots of bad thoughts about bad things will pass through our mind everyday, like flipping past television channels or fast-forwarding a CD, but the Bible says we can make the choice where we will stop and think for a while.

How much negative talk would we ever relay about somebody else if we chose not to let those "bad-report" thoughts take up residence in our minds? How many things do we say, good *or* bad, that weren't first thoughts? Our words don't just come out of nowhere. (Let's not let our husbands comment on that statement.)

Things that discourage us, depress us, bring us down, scare us, worry us and make us dissatisfied also make us feel like the world is a bad place to be. Negativism inside our minds creates in us a gloomy, dark outlook that can cause us to miss the pleasure and joy and beauty and wonder that just being alive, and having life in Jesus Christ, brings us. And we can die a thousand unnecessary deaths over things that will probably never happen.

We need to live every day in confidence as believers, while savoring and treasuring every precious moment, every precious relationship, every precious opportunity God graciously gives us that day, that week, that moment. What if we live every day like it might be our last, and then we live to be ninety? We will have absolutely maximized every wonderful day God has given to us. What a great life we'll look back on.

We can consciously take those bad-report thoughts and turn them into good-report thinking. For instance, we may pass a very boisterous or very sullen, very pierced, very tattooed, very unattractive, unappealing person in the mall or on the street. As critical thoughts fill our mind and we're just about to come out with some judgmental comment, we can, *right then,* in our mind thank the Lord for that person of supreme worth, and pray for God's direction, intervention, and blessing in their lives.

We are to see people as Jesus does, not condescendingly, but with the compassion and eternal insight that he expressed toward the

Samaritan woman at the well—as he saw in her a thirst much deeper than the sparkling water from the well could ever quench.

We are so blessed to know Jesus, the source of life-giving water, who loves all of us equally, no matter how we look or what we've done. We are to think about things that are of good report.

Fourth: Be Gracious/Be Real

The fourth thing God asks of us is to be gracious and real.

At least two thoughts come to mind here. The first is found in Matthew 7:1, "Do to others as you would have them do to you." We often teach the Golden Rule to our children in the same sort of ho-hum way as we might say, "An apple a day keeps the doctor away." But, in reality, we have a wonderful opportunity to model for them, and our coworkers, family and friends what it means in real life.

How do *we* want someone to talk to us? In a cranky, crabby tone? Do we want their words and body language to send a sarcastic, critical message? Do we want other people to avoid or ignore us? Do we want them to relate to us condescendingly? Most likely, we want their conversations with us to be kind, fair, loving, and complimentary.

When we lived in Seattle, we were acquainted with a wonderful family. Three generations lived together in a large home they had adapted to meet everyone's unique needs. Living upstairs in a garage apartment were the elderly grandparents. A daughter asked the grandmother once, jokingly, "What do you think about the devil, Mother?" Even on this topic the lady refused to sound critical. "My, he sure has been busy lately, hasn't he?" When she died nobody could remember her saying a word of criticism about anyone, ever.

In addition, how do we want people to look at us? None of us enjoys dirty looks or rolled eyes. We want people to see the "real" us that is underneath whatever the outside looks like. We want to be equally loved on bad-hair days or just after a trip to the hairdresser.

Hidden cameras in the home are a trend now. People have started to videotape their babysitter. How different would your behavior be if you knew it was being filmed? Believers practicing the task of being gracious don't have anything to worry about.

The second thought under this fourth multi-task of being gracious and real is found in Romans 12:9, "Let love be without hypocrisy" (NASB). The *New International Version* translates the verse succinctly: "Love must be sincere." I've learned a lot about that subject from my children, as you probably have from yours. My daughter, Lisa, loved to give things she had to other children. Often what she wanted to give to them didn't meet with my adult approval. Her generosity extended far beyond mine to things that were really special to her: her nicest necklace, her favorite doll, her stuffed animal. I thought she should give away those toys she didn't play with anymore, the clothes she never wore.

God convicted my self-focused heart when I remembered that Jesus gave his very best—that's what his kind of love does. I watched many a "treasure" leave her room over the years to take up residence in somebody else's home, and learned anew to be gracious, to be "real," from my dear child.

Fifth: Be a Servant

The fifth thing God asks us to do, as we spiritually multi-task, is to be a servant. Maybe when we hear those words we think, "I've got that one down; I'm a slave." Pick up this, tie that, wash this, clean this, cook that, start this, stop that, our daily tasks seem endless sometimes.

A number of years ago, my husband gave me a wonderful gift: he hired a house cleaner. Interestingly, she was a professional woman, highly educated and trained in other career positions, but she was also a devoted Christian and said that God had convicted her of her "unservantlike" spirit. She decided to do "service" work for someone else, to do jobs they needed done, but didn't especially like to do themselves. (It was a wonderful time in my life, I will have to admit.)

Paul teaches us in Galatians 5:13 (NIV) to "serve one another in love." Jesus describes to us in Luke 17:9–10 what a servant looks like after he (or she) has performed "servant duties." He explains that a servant, "is not even thanked, because he is merely doing what he is supposed to do. In the same way, when you obey me, you should say, 'We are not worthy of praise. We are servants who have simply done our duty.'" Is that hard for us to do? If you're like I am, yes.

We are to live and serve like Jesus Christ did, to think more highly of others than ourselves, "in honor preferring one another." Jesus said that if somebody takes your coat, give him your shirt also. He also said to turn the other cheek and go the second mile. James said that if we think we are something when we are really nothing, we deceive ourselves.

Being a servant isn't being subservient. You may ask, does that mean we're supposed to nurture a poor self-image and let others take advantage of us? Does that please God? Not at all! Over and over the Bible emphasizes the value God puts on us. The Lord of all the universe treasures you, me, and those who matter so much to us. He demonstrates our worth through the beautiful verbal descriptions found in the Psalms:

> "He is our God forever and ever and he will be our God until we die."
>
> (Psalm 48:14)

> "You are my strength; I wait for you to rescue me, for you, O God, are my place of safety. In his unfailing love, my God will come and help me."
>
> (Psalm 59:9–10)

> "The Lord says . . . 'When they call on me, I will answer; I will be with them in trouble, I will rescue them and honor them.'"
>
> (Psalm 91:15)

David gathers up descriptions from everyday life and creates a word picture from them to help us better understand God's magnificent love for us. From a heart full of gratitude, he exclaims in the Psalms:

> "O Lord, you have examined my heart and know everything about me. You know when I sit down or stand up. You know my every thought when far away. You chart the path ahead of me and tell me where to stop and rest. Every moment you know where I am. You know what I am going to say even before I say it, Lord. You both precede and follow me. You place your hand of blessing on my head. You saw me before I was born. Every day of my life was recorded in your book . . . How precious are your thoughts about me, O God! They are innumerable!"

> (Psalm 139:1–5, 16–17)

In addition to the incredible affirmation that we are valued by the living God, we also have an advocate—a God-appointed attorney, a representative of our best interests—in Jesus Christ. He takes up our cause when we've been taken advantage of as we serve him. He sees when we're unfairly treated. He hears every unkind confrontation, every demeaning expression. In his perfect timing, as a part of his polishing-us-up-plan to make us more like Jesus, he deals with the situation. With one precise chip of his Master Sculptor's chisel, he works to bring those who unfairly cause us suffering into a relationship with him that will change them, and make them able to receive God's blessing.

Becoming a servant is a choice. Servants sometimes suffer. Jesus Christ served and suffered and we are not greater than he. Our decision to serve him and then others gives us far more blessings than we can imagine.

So it comes down to this: if we're offended at the thought of serving someone, our husband, our boss, our mother-in-law, our child, our parent, our friend, our obnoxious neighbor, maybe there's a problem somewhere in our relationship with the servant of all servants; Jesus, the King.

Dr. Paul Brand is a highly respected and skilled surgeon and writer of the inspiring book, *Fearfully and Wonderfully Made*, coauthored by Phillip Yancey. Dr. Brand's amazing ability to transform people's lives through the gift of plastic and reconstructive surgery could have earned him vast monetary rewards, had he chosen to invest his healing skills and notable reputation exclusively in the lives of the "rich and famous." However, instead of capitalizing upon the personal advantages available through his amazing giftedness in reconstructing disfigured faces, broken bodies, damaged limbs and hands, Dr. Brand chose to live the life of a servant as he ministered to impoverished, hopeless, and helpless leprosy patients in India.

Nothing positive that our hands find to do need be considered drudgery, a waste of our precious time; we can choose to do it for Jesus because he gave us the hands, the mind, the body, the time, and the opportunity to do it.

As we commit everything we do unto God because we love him, no task will be too big or small, too ordinary, or too menial. No person performing these jobs will be any less important than anyone else, because everything we do is service to him; energy and time well-spent.

> Commit everything you do to the Lord. Trust him and he will help you.
>
> (Psalm 37:5)

> Commit your work to the Lord, and then your plans will succeed.
>
> (Proverbs 16:3)

I can commit my work as a parent to the Lord, and it will succeed. I can commit my work as a wife to the Lord, and it will succeed. I can commit my work in my job to the Lord, and it will succeed.

I can do these things not because I want to "look good," but because I'm doing it for the Lord. Even if outwardly these efforts don't look successful—our marriage crumbles or we lose our job—we are still victorious. In the Lord, we are a success. How it plays out or looks to other people doesn't matter, even if we never get a compliment or a job promotion. God sees our work and our commitment to him and is honored.

Doing whatever we do for Jesus is an expression of our belief that he is satisfied with us and our efforts. He will make something wonderful come from it, even if it turns out differently than we might have wished. And if we can't bring ourselves to commit our work to him, that "work" may need to be cast aside for something else he directs us to do. Paul tells us, "Whatever you do in word or deed, do all in the name of the Lord Jesus, giving thanks through Him to God the Father" (Colossians 3:17 NAS).

How many demanding tasks are you juggling right now? When one job on your to-do list gets erased, are three more waiting to be added? Do you sometimes feel like that "must-accomplish" list has taken on a life of its own, crying out to you, clamoring for your attention, trying to add one more thing to your plate that is already piled too high?

Your list may not look like mine, but the specific "what" that our hands find to do is not nearly as important as ensuring that our single focus is on Jesus Christ. When Jesus is the center of our life, our goals, and our daily endeavors, the time we spend and the energy we expend will be productive and significant, both now and for all eternity.

The Lord will provide the wisdom we need to take a fresh look at that seemingly all-important list we carry in our hearts and minds. He will help us "accentuate the positive and eliminate the negative" and maybe completely replace all the things we think we must *do*, with *who* he wants us to be.

Chapter 1 Study Questions

1. Spend time this week analyzing your single focus on the presence of Jesus in your life. What responsibilities, activities, interests, distractions or attention-absorbers make it most difficult for you to consistently focus on him? Ask the Lord to provide the insight, wisdom, and skill to accomplish your responsibilities in "real life," *and* to give Jesus his rightful position in your daily focus.

2. Discover which items on your spiritual "to be" list come most easily for you, or are consistently a part of who you are. Ask the Lord to continue to give you his power to be all that he desires, and thank him for the strength he gives you each day to live for him. As you acknowledge the strengths you see in your life, reaffirm to him, and to yourself, that you know that everything good in you comes from him, and thank him.

3. Submit yourself to the scrutiny of the Holy Spirit, and ask him to show you the qualities on God's "to be" list that he wants to establish or develop more fully and consistently in your life. Begin this week to make changes where they are needed, even in small increments, and be available daily to the Lord to make you everything he desires for you "to be."

4. Since the "to be" qualities we discussed in this study were not an exhaustive list, has God brought to your mind other important characteristics that you want him to manifest in your life?

5. If you would like to do a personal study using this chapter's topic, here are some Scriptures you may want to refer to:

Single-Focus	Spiritual "Multi-Tasking"
Psalm 11:7; 16:5, 8	Proverbs 31
John 1:14	Matthew 7:12
1 Corinthians 8:4, 6	2 Corinthians 2:14; 9:15
2 Corinthians 12:5	Galatians 5:13
Ephesians 4:4–6	Ephesians 6:10–17
Philippians 3:13	Philippians 2:14; 4:8
1 Timothy 2:5	Colossians 3:2
Hebrews 10:12	1 Timothy 6:6
James 1:8	1 Thessalonians 5:17
	James 1:2–4; 3:17

Be Tolerant/Intolerant

Lisa

I grew up as a pastor's daughter. According to my calculations, by the time I graduated from high school we had moved approximately ten times and lived in seven states. I went on to college and then graduate school in two more states and in different time zones. So yes, I have moved a lot, and you would think I am used to it by now. I'm not. Packing, cleaning, saying goodbye, unpacking, cleaning, finding a new church, changing our address on everything from bills, to subscriptions, to the IRS—I don't like it a bit.

Research shows that moving is one of the top five most stressful things a person can experience, and I believe it. And if you move from one state to another, you get the biggest whammy of them all; you must pay a visit to a very unpleasant place. Just its initials give me a stomachache; the DMV. The Department of Motor Vehicles. (Perhaps your state calls it something else, but it's still a nightmare.)

There's no way around it; if you want a driver's license you must tolerate the demands of the DMV.

We know that God asks us as women to be able to both multi-task and be focused. What else does he expect of us? This chapter's topic is not one that may at first come to mind, but it is something all women, regardless of their situation in life, deal with everyday. God asks a woman to be tolerant *and* intolerant.

God Asks Women To Be Tolerant

"Tolerance." That's a ten-dollar word. What does it mean?

When I think of the word, I can't help but think of a schoolmarm from "Little House on the Prairie" days in a bun and thick spectacles addressing a rowdy student. "I will not tolerate that kind of behavior in this classroom!"

You could probably think of all kinds of unpleasant things you just can't tolerate: fingernails on a blackboard, people cutting in line, talking on cell phones in a restaurant, raunchy shows on TV. Yet there are some unpleasant things we tolerate everyday and don't give much thought to: traffic, fad diets, doctor appointments, family get-togethers.

Go back to those long lines at the DMV. Why do we put up with them? We endure difficult situations and experiences because of what we get from them when they're over. That's called motivation. Tolerance is really all about what motivates you.

The Motivation Behind Tolerance

I have to admit, with some hesitation, that I have watched the TV show *Fear Factor*. People do the most bizarre things on national TV. The absolute worst things I've witnessed on this show either involve eating things that no human person should ever put in their body, or enduring getting up close and personal with our slimy amphibian or six-legged friends. In a recent episode, the contestants allowed themselves to become entombed in a very small Plexiglas box locked with a large heavy chain while the host and his assistants poured buckets of spiders over their face and body.

You know that under normal circumstances, these men and women would be "creeped out" by one tiny spider crawling on them, much less all over. Yet here they are willingly psyching themselves up to do these stunts, and when it's all over they yell, "Oh yeah!" and give everyone smiles and high fives. Why? Because they are motivated. They know that there is a huge pay-off for the one who finishes first. How huge? Fifty thousand dollars huge.

You and I may not be motivated to undergo such torture, but all of us are motivated to do things in life. We're motivated by fame and fortune and future, and things we think we need and things we want to gain. So, we tolerate some things we should, some things we just have to, and some things that probably aren't so great.

Let's say you promised me a gift card to the Target store if I would jump off a boat in the middle of the ocean in the coldest month of winter. As much as I love Target, I would have to say "thanks but no thanks." But if my family happened to be out in a boat, in the middle of the ocean, in the winter, and one of my three children fell into that cold water, you can bet your life that in a split second I would jump right in without hesitation. And I would stay out there as long as it took to save them.

My motivation to tolerate the conditions around me would be the value I place on my children. When God created us he put a value on us. Remember Genesis 1:27? Fortunately, he did not give us varying degrees of value; he created all of us in his image. Otherwise, we might pale in comparison to the apostle Paul or Abraham or Job, or other heroes of the faith. We are told, "So God created man in his own image, in the image of God he created him; male and female he created them."

He also created us all for the same purpose and because of the same reason: "To do good works, which God prepared in advance for us to do" (Ephesians 2:10 NIV).

What do you think of when you think of good works? Perhaps you think of loving your family and friends, praying for people, going to church, tithing, reading your Bible. Those certainly would be included in this category, but what else does he ask us to do?

God asks us to tolerate some specific things. We're going to look at two broad categories and their implications.

Being Tolerant: Of People

The first category of tolerance contains the relational aspects of life; in a nutshell, people. We're talking about the people in our life, people we come in contact with, people who don't necessarily think like us, smell like us, act like us, or even believe like us. The relational aspects of life are not always cut and dried; they can sometimes be difficult and tricky.

For example, if someone you know is clearly living in sin according to the Bible, such as practicing homosexuality, are we to tolerate that sin and embrace the sin of homosexuality? No. Of course not. But what about the relational aspect of it? Should we, and can we, tolerate the person while rejecting the sin itself? Yes. They are, after all, two separate issues.

If I asked you to list three things that define you as a person—things that make you who you are—most of you would probably list things like mother, friend, wife, Christian, daughter, American, nurse, stay-at-home-mom, sister, executive, and so on. But you would not list your sins. You wouldn't introduce yourself to someone you just met by saying, "Hi, I'm Sue. I tell lies and don't read my Bible very much and am addicted to gambling. Nice to meet you." Our sin is not who we are. Never doubt that you are loved and accepted by your Creator at the very same time that the sin in your life is rejected by him.

46

In his eyes, you and I and all the people we meet are in the same boat. We're sinful, and we're loved by God. Therefore, we are to value all people, because he values us. And we're not just to tolerate them like the barking dog next door that we try to put up with by ignoring it. We are to connect with them, to empathize with them, to care about them.

The Bible is riddled with situations and scenarios where God himself got personally involved in the lives of people that other people wouldn't touch with a ten-foot pole. Remember the woman at the well? In John 4 we're told how she was a Samaritan woman and Jesus was a Jew. In those days, Jews did not associate with Samaritans. End of story. Yet he asked her for a drink. Was it because he didn't know who she was? No, he knew. By his action, he was making a statement.

How about the woman caught in adultery who was to be stoned (John 8:1–11)? After writing with his finger in the sand, Jesus said to her loud and rowdy accusers, "He who is without sin among you, let him throw a stone at her first" (v 7 NKJV). By his words, he was making a point.

Or consider the woman who was a sinner (the scripture didn't say what kind of sin) who anointed the feet of Jesus to the scorn of those who witnessed it (Luke 7:36–50). By his acceptance, he was making an impact.

How about Zacchaeus? People hated him because he was a dreaded tax collector. Yet Jesus asked Zacchaeus to let him be a guest in his home. By his request, he was making a difference.

Or the man with leprosy in Mark 1:40–45. Jesus touched him, and the man was miraculously healed. By his boldness, he was changing a life.

Paul, whose name was changed from Saul, had been a persecutor of Christians. Not a really desirable guy. But don't you think God may have used him, and the other apostles and disciples, as examples because he knew we would be able to identify with them? They, like us in our era of corruption, were sinners in dire need of a savior.

Here's a hypothetical situation for you. A man holds a woman hostage in a domestic dispute. The police at the scene try to negotiate but to no avail. In the course of this terrible event both the woman and the man holding her hostage get shot. They are rushed to the same hospital, arriving at the same exact time. Who should be treated first?

A soldier and a terrorist lay next to each other in a makeshift hospital in the middle of the desert amid an ongoing war. Both are in dire need of medical attention and you're short of doctors. Who should be tended to first?

Our first reaction is to judge the offending party. We say that he should get what's coming to him. He was the one in the wrong, he did this to himself, he deserves it. So treat the innocent party first and let the perpetrator get his just desserts.

Not so with God. To him, "all have sinned and fall short of the glory of God" (Romans 3:23). Therefore, we must value everyone and be tolerant of them, just as Christ himself has been oh-so-tolerant of us. And remember, James says this:

> My brothers, as believers in our glorious Lord Jesus Christ, don't show favoritism. Suppose a man comes into your meeting wearing a gold ring and fine clothes, and a poor man in shabby clothes also comes in. If you show special attention to the man wearing fine clothes and say, "Here's a good seat for you," but say to the poor man, "you stand there" or "sit on the floor by my feet," have you not discriminated among yourselves and become judges with evil thoughts? . . . If you really keep the royal law found in Scripture, "Love your neighbor as yourself," you are doing right. But if you show favoritism, you sin and are convicted by the law as lawbreakers. For whoever keeps the whole law and yet stumbles at just one point is guilty of breaking all of it.
>
> (James 2:1–4, 8–10 NIV)

But many of us don't like to do this. It bothers us too much. Maybe it's because what we see in them reminds us of our own sin and depravity. We want to reject both the sin and the sinner and let their sin define who they are as people. We have become so intolerant of people that we see them through a lens of judgment and we hardly value them at all.

That's not what God asks of us. One of the hardest things God asks a woman to do is be tolerant of the people in her life.

Being Tolerant: Of Circumstances

There's more. Sometimes God asks us to tolerate the situational aspects of life. In other words, circumstances. They may be circumstances he puts us in to serve as a testimony to others for his honor and glory. They may be a loss of something or someone, a major illness, an unending painful situation, or some other scenario. These situations may be no fun.

When you encounter salespeople, do you want them to sell you a product they have never tried? Do you want waiters to recommend a dish they have never tasted? Of course not. We want firsthand experience when it comes to these things, and that is true of most things in life. If a woman comes to you and says that she is struggling with an issue—let's say infertility problems—and you yourself have been in that same difficult situation, you can identify with that woman. It's easier for you to say the right words and feel for her and encourage her at her point of need than it is for someone who hasn't been through it.

But let's say you have a friend who is suffering from lupus. You have never had lupus or known anyone with it. You may pray with her, love her, share Scripture with her, and help her with whatever she needs. But as hard as you try, you cannot tell her that you know how she feels, that you have been there.

The Bible provides awesome words that help us gain the perspective we need to tolerate our circumstances, whatever they may be.

49

For instance, in 2 Corinthians 4:8–9 (NIV), Paul says "We are hard pressed on every side, but not crushed; perplexed, but not in despair; persecuted, but not abandoned; struck down, but not destroyed." He continues in verses 16–18 this way:

> Therefore we do not lose heart. Though outwardly we are wasting away, yet inwardly we are being renewed day by day. For our light and momentary troubles are achieving for us an eternal glory that far out-weighs them all. So we fix our eyes not on what is seen, but on what is unseen. For what is seen is temporary, but what is unseen is eternal.

The apostle Peter also acknowledges this process: "And the God of all grace, who called you to his eternal glory in Christ, after you have suffered a little while, will himself restore you and make you strong, firm and steadfast" (1 Peter 5:10 NIV).

As Peter teaches us, God sometimes asks us to tolerate a circumstance that won't defeat us, but does stretch us in such a way that we can grow to a greater understanding of who he is in our lives. He uses these trials to help us better identify with people, empathize with people, love them, encourage them, and tell them about the power of God.

Remember, Jesus knows your circumstance and shares your pain. He cares for you and will not let you slip out of his grasp. Know this: If God asks you to tolerate a tough situation in life, he will surely see you through it. Jesus prepared his disciples for persecution with these words:

> Do not be afraid of those who kill the body but cannot kill the soul. Rather, be afraid of the One who can destroy both soul and body in hell. Are not two sparrows sold for a penny? Yet not one of them will fall to the ground apart from the will of your Father. And even the very hairs of your head are all numbered. So don't be afraid; you are worth more than many sparrows.

> (Matthew 10:28–31 NIV)

We've established the *who* (people) and the *what* (circumstances). Of course we also must mention the *why*. Why should we be motivated to tolerate these people and circumstances? It's pretty basic, really. As followers of Christ, whom he created for his glory, whom he formed and made, whose name we are given; we are to be motivated for one very specific reason in life: To serve and honor the Lord every day that we live.

That's not all he asks us to do, though. God asks us to do something else that is very difficult. He asks us to be *intolerant* of some things.

God Asks Us To Be Intolerant

Millions of people in the world have a common medical condition called lactose intolerance. The body cannot digest lactose, the primary sugar in cow's milk. Babies afflicted with it drink a specialized formula, and adults suffering from it can't pick up a regular gallon of milk at the store. God asks us to be intolerant of sin in much the same way. Instead of being unable to consume a milk product, we are to have the inability to "digest" sin.

But what kind of sin? The sin we see in the lives of others? Sadly, we have that one down pat most of the time. Yes, we should reject all sin, but we are talking about something much more personal. God is asking us to be intolerant of sin in our own life. No lying, cheating or stealing allowed. No committing adultery or committing fraud. No angry attitudes. Doesn't that about sum it all up in the sin category? What else can there be? How about gossip, self-focus, fear, and mediocrity?

These are some of the sins we don't pay much attention to, ones that often slip through our fingers and slide into our lives. But their effect is greater than we might naively think. Let's take a closer look.

Being Intolerant: Of Gossip

Ever heard someone say they wanted to "share something in love"? You may hear a different code phrase for gossip in your circles but the effect is the same.

And the most notorious setting for gossip? In a small group setting or prayer group of women. You've probably been there. You are sitting down and someone begins to mention a "prayer request" with these words: "Now, I am just sharing this in love . . ." and she proceeds to unleash a beast of news about so-and-so we need to pray for, and why. She uses the words "sharing in love" as a disclaimer of what she's getting ready to say so people will know her "true" motives right up front. I'm sure some of the time someone *is* sincerely sharing something in love, but so often phrases like this are nothing more than a cover-up for the sin of gossip.

Gossip is such a problem for us, isn't it? It's as if we women were born with an extra chromosome: the XXG (for gossip) (I'm stepping on my own toes here). We despise it in others but tolerate it in ourselves. We convince ourselves that what we are talking about has merit. We act sincere, or just act without thinking, because we have tolerated it so much in the past it's not even a thought in our minds anymore.

Jesus asks us to become intolerant of gossip in our own lives. After all, the first twelve verses in the third chapter of the book of James are devoted to the very tool we use to execute this sin: the silly, slithery tongue. And talk about word pictures. James compared the tongue to a forest fire, a horse's bit, a fig tree, a giant ship and a saltwater spring. Your tongue, when unregulated, is a natural disaster. That's no small thing.

When I was in graduate school, the apartment complex I lived in caught on fire. I experienced firsthand just how fast and furious a fire can spread. Fortunately, no one lost their life that day, but for those who lost belongings or the shelter of their home, it was devastating. Destruction abounds when the mighty fury of a fire, tsunami, earthquake, tornado or hurricane, destroys everything in its path. And the same is true of gossip. It damages and devastates.

A boy named Johnny and his family lived in a small town. Everyone knew his father was an alcoholic. Johnny was a good boy, but the town kids would tease him because they heard their parents talking about his situation. One day, one of the kids at church found a can of beer in a closet at the church. He took it to one of the leaders. "Who does this belong to?" the leader asked. The boy guessed. "It might belong to Johnny. You know, his daddy has a drinking problem and all."

The church leaders decided Johnny shouldn't be around the others kids at church anymore so they asked him to leave. Of course word got out that Johnny wasn't going to church anymore because of his drinking. The principal called him and expelled him. Johnny tried to reason with the principal and defend himself, but the principal wouldn't listen.

Some time later Johnny went by one of his old friends' house to see if he could come out and play catch. The friend's mother answered the door. "I'm sorry, son, but my boy is not allowed to play with you anymore," she said. "Go on home."

Johnny was devastated by all of this. He hadn't done anything wrong. He couldn't help it that his daddy was an alcoholic. But he couldn't defend himself against all the townspeople who were convinced he had done something he hadn't. A few days later, Johnny's mother came in from working out in the fields. She called out for Johnny but got no reply. Finally, she went to the back of the house and found Johnny hanging from a tree with a noose around his neck.

He was still breathing, though, and she got him down and to the hospital. As he lay hooked up to a ventilator, alive but brain-damaged, just one person visited. The church janitor. "Ma'am," he said to Johnny's mother, with tears in his eyes, "I'm sorry about Johnny. He was a good boy. The truth is, it's my fault that all this happened. See, I am the one who brought the beer to church. I was afraid I'd lose my job if I told anyone about it, so I kept my mouth shut. I heard all the talking and the rumors, but I let people think Johnny had done it because I didn't think it would matter. I'm so sorry."

A forest fire. A natural disaster. Gossip. God is asking us as Christian women to be intolerant of gossip in our lives. He's asking us to set aside our own agendas and insecurities, which cause us to spread gossip about others.

Jesus says in 1 Timothy 6:20–21 (NIV), "Turn away from godless chatter and the opposing ideas of what is falsely called knowledge, which some have professed and in so doing have wandered from the faith." By rejecting gossip, we tolerate the needs and inadequacies of others.

Being Intolerant: Of a Focus on the Self

As a young girl, I loved watching the Muppets. They were (and are) cute, silly, and appealing creatures (remember Gonzo?) who joked their way into both television and the movies. My favorite character was the one and only Miss Piggy. I had posters up in my room, not of Shawn Cassidy or Debbie Boone but of Miss Piggy. She dressed impeccably and was so beautiful and clever and irresistible—just ask her. Poor Kermit the Frog ("Kermy") was completely overshadowed by her. Not only that, he couldn't get a word in edgewise because she was always talking so much—about herself. "Now enough about *me*," she would say, with a flourish, "what do *you* think about me?"

Ever known any real Miss Piggys? Those I have encountered made me feel as if, even when they were asking about me, it was really still all about them. The truth is that most of us are like Miss Piggy to some degree. We may not be narcissistic Muppets, but we have a hard time grasping the concept of *others before self*. My needs. My wants. My life. Me, myself, and I.

Like Miss Piggy, for many women, self-focus is manifested in extreme self-love and narcissism. God requires us to not tolerate it. Romans 12:3 tells us, "Do not think of yourself more highly than you ought, but rather think of yourself with sober judgment, in accordance with the measure of faith God has given you." Galatians 6:3 carries it a step further, "If anyone thinks he is something when he is nothing, he deceives himself." Narcissistic self-focus is a very destructive tool of Satan to move us away from our mission in life, which is to serve and honor God by serving and loving others.

God admonishes us in Proverbs 11:25 (NIV) by saying, "A generous man will prosper; he who refreshes others will himself be refreshed." We cannot possibly be generous with others if we are focusing all our efforts on ourselves. And not just generous in action, but also with our attitude.

Sometimes the attitude is subtle. Here's an example. A woman gets a call from out-of-town friends who are coming for a visit. All the woman can think about is how much time and effort it's going to take to clean the house, shop for food, host her guests, and get the house whipped back into shape after they're gone. By the time the friends get there, the joy of them coming is overshadowed by the stress of hosting them.

It's the Martha mentality versus the Mary mentality. Remember the story? Mary visited with Jesus while Martha scurried around, perfecting things, brooding all the time at how much work she was doing. How much did Martha miss out on because of her self-focus? Sure, she wanted things to be nice and just so for her Lord, but she was, in a very real way, thinking about herself and how she would appear to Jesus.

Self-love is not the only way a woman can have an unhealthy inward focus. Self-loathing, or self-hatred, can also result from this sin, and it is just as destructive, maybe even more so. Self-hatred can take on many different forms and has many faces. Being a part of today's culture means being constantly bombarded with images of people much more beautiful than we are: with shapelier legs, silkier hair, and flatter abs. We worship youth and disregard, even discard, our elders. Secular society touts women as mere objects for a man's physical and sexual satisfaction, holding no real value in virtue or purity. We have bought into the lie, and we hate ourselves because of it.

One such dangerous "self-loathing" trend is that of "cutting." I actually happen to have a friend who is a cutter. Cutters use knives, razor blades, or some other sharp object on their bodies to inflict pain. The act somehow dulls or releases their inner pain and self-hatred, making them feel more alive. Unfortunately, this form of self-mutilation is growing, mostly among young women. I don't understand all the whys attached to this bizarre practice, but the sad truth is that cutters hate themselves so much that they can think of no better way to express it than by harming their very own flesh.

The Word of God tells us that we are to not only accept but to embrace the woman he made us to be. Psalm 139 is a chapter of gratefulness to God, essentially a poetic thank-you for creating me just like God wanted me to be. Verse 14 says, "I will praise you, Lord, for I am fearfully and wonderfully made." It is in this attitude of gratitude that we learn to recognize the unique and special child of God we are, and, in so doing, break the bondage of sin and self. We are who we are because that is exactly who he created us to be.

I grew up in the home of one of the most godly of all women. Truthfully, my mother is the ultimate Proverbs 31 woman and everything else. (And I'm not just saying this because we are writing this book together!) I am blessed to have her not only as my mom, but also my role model, spiritual mentor, and friend. From the time I was very young, my friends were telling me how lucky I was to have such an awesome mom. And they were right.

But it wasn't always easy. For one thing, when you are the daughter of someone beautiful, gracious, loving, giving, kind, and ever-so-gentle, well, that is a somewhat intimidating standard to try to measure up to. Especially when you are not exactly wired the same way. She is the Mary Poppins to my Joan of Arc (I've always been dramatic). I am the bull in her china shop, and we both know it.

I spent a lot of years trying to be more like my mother. Many times I wished I had been created to be more like her than I was. As a younger woman, it was especially difficult for me because I felt like I wanted to be someone else, but that wasn't what God had intended for me at all. See, in a very real way, by wanting to be someone else, I wasn't loving the Lisa that God had created. I was rejecting his creative genius of crafting the human being with a Type A personality and headstrong ways. I was a work in progress, to be sure, but I was his "workmanship." And as I matured in my faith, I began to realize that God knew what he was doing when he made me. I let go of the pipe dream of becoming my mother, and at the same time, embraced the reality of who I was—in Christ. I decided that if God had created me with a loud voice, I should use it to speak out for him. If I was a strong-minded woman, with the help of God, I could channel that strength into influencing others to live more God-centered, purposeful lives. I realized that it was okay to be who I was, so long as I let the mighty hand of God shape me into the "me" I needed to be. And to my surprise, I began to like myself a whole lot more.

Just like a tight rope walker, we must learn to balance ourselves with prayer and the proper perspective of who we really are. Whether in the form of self-love or self-loathing, we must be intolerant of the "me factor" in our lives. Because here's the truth: not tolerating the sin of self-focus allows us to better tolerate those around us.

Being Intolerant: Of Fear

The beach is one of my favorite places to be on earth. I don't like the sand so much, especially with three small children and all they can do with it. But I love the water. I love to hear its mighty roar as it crashes onto the shore. And I love to watch my children play in it, laughing and splashing while they try to "outrun" the waves.

Several years ago my husband and I took Graham, our only child at the time, to the beach for a few days. He was excited to get there and play, and I was anxious to rest my eight-months-pregnant feet on the soft sand while my husband and child got some daddy-son time. I only watched them for a few minutes before drifting off to sleep in my brightly-colored beach chair. I didn't see the events of the next few minutes, but my husband remembers them quite vividly.

The beach we were visiting was right on an Intracoastal Waterway. The enormous cargo ships would pass by at a certain time everyday. And for a two-year-old child, the "great big boat" was possibly the neatest thing he had ever seen in his young life. Graham was ecstatic. "Wook, Daddy," he said, "See the big boat?" "Yes, buddy, I see it." My husband was thrilled to share the moment with his awestruck son.

But pretty soon, my husband noticed that the undertow was starting to pull them out a little farther than he felt comfortable going. The power of the big boat had made quite an impact on the ocean water. While Graham continued to play, my husband became afraid. "Let's go back in, closer to Mommy, okay?" His anxiety was intensifying as the subtle tug of water got stronger. As a young child, Graham was oblivious. Soon Daddy's words became commanding. "Come on, big guy, it's time to go in now. Hold on to me, and I'll carry you back to the shore." With that, he scooped up our son and Graham wrapped his arms around his neck. He was holding on to his daddy, and his daddy was holding on to him. Nothing or no one could have come between them.

Life is unpredictable, and dangers loom closer than we may sometimes think. Undertows can sweep our feet from under us without warning, but our God is ready, willing, and able to scoop us up into his arms, his mighty arms, and carry us to a place of shelter, safety, and ultimate security. Isaiah 12:2 tells us, "See, God has come to save me. I will trust in him and not be afraid." It says in 1 John 4:18 that "perfect love expels all fear." Since no one is perfect but our Heavenly Father, we can safely conclude that "perfect love" can only come from him. He is our source, the only one we need to rid us of all our deep anxieties and concerns. We must rely on him, and him alone, to save us.

I learned a verse when I was a young child: "What time I am afraid, I will trust in Thee." It started out as just one of the weekly verses that my mother made me memorize to get a star on my "good behavior chart." But Psalm 56:3 came to mean so much more. I would recall this verse whenever I started to feel scared because it was dark or if I'd had a bad dream. I said it when I thought I heard a noise or if I imagined a "bad guy" in my room. It helped me go back to sleep feeling less afraid. With years of life now under my belt and young children of my own, I am still quoting this verse. Gone are the days of the boogeyman, but I still get scared; I get scared about my health, I get scared for my children, and I get scared about what tomorrow holds. And when I do, I recite those ten precious and inspired words that seem as though they were written just for me. They help me not to be so afraid when the darkness comes.

When you are facing your fear, whatever it is, God is asking you to hold on to him. He in turn will hold on to you. And nothing and no one will ever come between you.

Being Intolerant: Of Mediocrity

I love to snow ski. Well, I *used* to love to snow ski, when I had extra time and money and fewer responsibilities in life. I grew up in the Midwest, and every year my youth group would charter a bus and go skiing for three days, and my older brother and I would go almost every year.

After learning the basics, and with a few years of practice, I convinced myself that I was ready to tackle a challenge. In Colorado the slopes marked with black diamonds are the most advanced (and life-threatening) trails at a ski resort. Black diamonds are for the most elite skiers on the hill. Or, in my case, the most overconfident.

So I decided this was the year of Lisa and the black diamond slope! I've always enjoyed challenges, but there was another motive behind my desire to ski this slope. Anyone who skied a black diamond slope received a free, black t-shirt with the words *No Fear* on it in bold letters. I wanted that t-shirt. It was a big deal, especially when you are in tenth grade and trying to be popular.

I announced my decision to my friends. My guy friends were especially thrilled that their prissy friend with pink nails and Aqua-Netted hair was going to do something gutsy for once. They gladly escorted me to the chair lift. Up we went, and went, and went. I found myself wondering, a) if this elevation was even legal, and b) if there was any other way down.

We finally got to our destination at the very, very top of the mountain. And this girl with "no fear" was starting to get just a tad bit fearful. But I wanted to save face and meet the challenge and get that free t-shirt. So I played it cool; I positioned my goggles, pulled down my hat, took a hard gulp and let gravity do its thing. Can I tell you that, other than the dreams in which I arrive at church with just my underwear on, I have never had such a feeling of horror in my whole life? I think on the way down I simultaneously felt like I broke a hip, lost my voice, took ten years off my life, *and* wet my pants! I just knew I was going to die, with no driver's license, wearing braces, a virgin, with no chance of ever having a baby.

But in what seemed like no time at all, I ended up at the bottom in one piece. Or should I say, one pile. I did it! I became the proud owner of a black t-shirt that said *No Fear*. Not only that, but also I gained a challenging and motivating experience in life.

No fear. No pain, no gain. The greater the risk, the greater the reward. We've heard all these slogans at one time or another. But what do they mean? And in particular, what do they mean to us as Christian women?

God asks us to be intolerant of mediocrity in our life. How does that look in real life? Mediocrity is living the status quo. It's playing it safe. It's settling. It's patronizing ourselves. It's excusing ourselves. It's fearing something so much that we are willing to never experience it and all its benefits in exchange for the safe comfort we already know. And as women, we have the tendency to relish our comfort zones.

Settling for safe can be sinful. Consider these verses. Deuteronomy 6:5 says, "Love the Lord with *all* your heart and with *all* your soul and with *all* your strength" (my emphasis). We are told in 1 Corinthians 10:31 to "do all things for the glory of God." In Revelation 3:15–16, Jesus addresses the church at Laodicea and says: "I know your deeds, that you are neither cold nor hot. I wish you were either one or the other! So, because you are lukewarm—neither hot nor cold—I am about to spit you out of my mouth."

This doesn't mean you should live your life recklessly, but it does mean that our mediocre ho-hum attitudes can hinder us in our walk with the Lord.

A few years ago my husband faced a personal challenge of his own by running in the New York City Marathon. I left our only child at the time with his grandparents and went with Scott to cheer him on. The New York City Marathon is known not only for its great athletes but also for its camaraderie, as the entire city comes out to support the runners.

On that cold November day I settled into my place behind the ropes and cleared my throat to prepare for my cheerleader role. I saw young people, old people, skinny people, very skinny people, heavy people, different nationalities—a true melting pot of people participating. Watching them I suddenly realized a great irony: though I came to cheer them on, instead of inspiring them, they were inspiring me. But it didn't stop there. I saw another group of runners who took me to the next level of inspiration. People with missing arms and legs, running or at the least walking to the finish line with everyone else. If anyone had an excuse not to run a marathon, this was the group. But they were out there, in the mix.

At that moment I felt like such an unmotivated person. Here I was, a woman in her twenties, with maybe a few pounds to lose but generally healthy, with all my limbs, and I had never even thought about doing such a difficult thing. I was settling into my comfortable position on the sidelines, and that was just fine with me.

Many of us are settling for the sidelines of life. We like our life the way it is, and we don't really want to mess it up. We don't really want the Lord to give us anything too hard to do. It's hard for many of us to even be willing to make time for nurturing our own spiritual walk through personal Bible study, much less spread the gospel and tell others about Christ's love, sacrifice, and forgiveness. But I firmly believe that our mediocre attitude towards areas like witnessing displeases the Lord and can cause us to have sin in our lives.

Women, our love for God and our desire to do his will should be enough to motivate us to get out of our comfort zones and ski the black diamonds of life. For the Christian woman, mediocrity is not an option. Living a life of mediocrity will cause us to miss out on the great things God has for us to experience.

Titus 3:14 says this, "Our people must learn to devote themselves to doing what is good, in order that they may provide for daily necessities and not live unproductive lives." God does not ask us to live unproductive lives. He asks us not to tolerate the status quo. Because not tolerating mediocrity, not taking the easy road, rocking that boat a little bit, will help us to not only live fuller and more meaningful lives, but also to fulfill his will for us while we are here on this earth.

On the Black Diamond Slopes of Life

My dear grandmother passed away in 2004. She was such a unique woman. In her way she skied the black diamonds of life. She was always giving people money, even though she was not a wealthy woman; in fact, she earned her living for almost thirty years in a department store, selling clothes. She was a woman with a bold witness. During her funeral, the family she left behind was deeply touched by the stories her friends, co-workers, and neighbors lined up to tell about her, how, in some way, Ernestine Reimer had touched their lives. My uncle shared a story about my grandmother I hadn't heard before. Here's what he said:

Mother was such a pure heart. She was a woman of great determination and faith, truly led by the Holy Spirit. One day I was sitting in my office and the phone rang. It was mother. She said, "Wade-O? [her nickname for him] Son, I need you to do a favor for me."

"Sure, Mom," I said.

She said, "I need you to take me to the hospital to see someone. I met him at the department store and sold him some clothes. He's sick and he's in the hospital and I need to go to him."

"Sure, Mom, when do you want to go?" I asked.

And she said, "God told me to go right now."

So my uncle drove across town in the busy Houston traffic, picked her up and drove her to the hospital. When they got to the person's room, they saw a shriveled up, sickly man dying of AIDS. He was alone. No family. No friends around him. Just the sound of the monitors and the smell of death. He was sweating profusely, and my dear grandmother went immediately to his side. She called the nurse and requested some ice and damp towels. And she began to serve this man she had just barely met by wiping down his broken body. And some time later, she turned to my uncle and said, "Wade, will you pray with him? He needs God." So my Uncle Wade, took this man's hand and prayed with him and explained to him about God and his love, and in that moment, Christ came to live inside his heart, and he was saved. And several hours later, the man went to be with his Lord.

My dear and godly grandmother knew that she had to do what God had asked her to do when he asked her to do it. And she was obedient to his call; skiing the black diamonds of life. Tolerating others. Enduring difficult circumstances. Being intolerant of our sin. God asks a woman to do some hard, hard things.

Chapter 2 Study Questions

1. Spend some time this week analyzing what things in your life you tolerate and why. Ask the Lord to provide the insight and wisdom to determine what things you should or should not tolerate (James 1:5).

2. Think about the people you interact with on a daily basis: family, co-workers, neighbors, friends, strangers. Determine your level of tolerance for each of them on a scale of 1 to 10 (1= low tolerance; 10 = high tolerance). Evaluate whether this tolerance level is pleasing to God. Ask the Lord to give you discernment and the eyes of grace to see these people as he sees them.

3. Submit yourself to the scrutiny of the Holy Spirit and ask him to show you the areas of your life you should be intolerant of. Make a list of the things you are tolerating that are hindering your walk. Give them over to God and claim the victory in your life over each and every area.

4. What are some ways you have been "playing it safe" in your life? Search your heart. Does living a life of mediocrity hinder God's plan for you and stifle you from what you should be doing? Ask the Lord to give you the desire and strength to be all he wants you to be.

5. If you would like to do a personal study using this chapter's topic, here are some Scriptures you may want to refer to:

Tolerance	Intolerance
Genesis 1:27	Deuteronomy 6:5
Mark 1	Proverbs 11:25
Luke 7	Matthew 12:30;
Romans 2:1; 3:23; 13:10;	Galatians 5:16–26
14:1–12	1 Corinthians 10:31
1 Corinthians 13	Ephesians 5:1–14
2 Corinthians 6:4–10; 12:7–10	Colossians 3:17
Galatians 2:6b; 5:14–15; 6:1–5	1 Timothy 6:20
Ephesians 2:10; 3:26–28; 4:2–3;	2 Timothy 2:22
5:9	James 4:14
Hebrews 6:10; 12:14	1 Peter 2:1
James 2:1–10	Revelation 3:15–16
1 Peter 2:17; 3:8; 4:8; 4:13–16	
1 John 2:10–11; 3:11–24;	
4:7–21	
Jude 20–22	

Fail/Succeed

Kathie

elcome to Failures Anonymous. We sneak in the backdoor and meet in the basement. Some of us are in disguise. We wear the masks of good performance, the many hats of admirable behavior, the coats of enviable credentials, and nice-gal necklaces.

I'm the leader of the bunch. Yes, I admit that I am a failure. Not I-used-to-be-a-failure-but-I-worked-hard-and-now-I'm-successful; no, I was born a chronic, repetitive failure. I was a failure as a student. I made mistakes on my papers and did assignments incorrectly—or even forgot to do them. I was a failure as a teacher. Not all my students got A's, and some didn't even move to the next grade. I'm a failure as a wife. I can't make my husband completely happy all the time. I'm a failure as a mom. I didn't love or discipline my children perfectly, and sometimes I let my children stay up late and have junk food, and even ate it with them. (I know, that's shocking, but it's true.) I'm a failure as a homemaker. I don't cook as often as I should and my house gets cluttered; my wastebaskets need emptying right now. I'm a failure as a speaker. I sometimes say the wrong things or am not as clear or organized as I should be. Sometimes the audience has no clue what I'm trying to say. I'm an absolute failure. Sometimes it's obvious to everyone. Sometimes I fail secretly and then try desperately to keep it hidden.

Are you a failure like me? Do you realize you are a card-carrying member of Failures Anonymous? I hope so. Not because misery loves company, but because that's really a good place for us to be.

Over the years, there have been many notable failures. Jonas Salk tried and failed two hundred times before discovering the polio vaccine. Asked if he felt his achievement compensated for all those attempts, Dr. Salk said he had never thought of them as failures but as discoveries on the road to his two hundred and first success.

Beethoven's teacher called him hopeless as a musician and composer. Walt Disney was fired from a local newspaper for his lack of creativity, and went bankrupt several times before Disneyland was created. Albert Einstein did not speak until he was four years old, and his teachers regarded him as "slow to learn." Babe Ruth hit 714 home runs but struck out 1,330 times. Henry Ford crashed financially five times before he launched the automotive business. Abraham Lincoln had more failures than successes, and even suffered a complete emotional breakdown. Still he did not give up.

Then there's the story of a guy named Sparky. He failed every subject in the eighth grade and did not do much better in high school. Social life was a disaster for him. Nobody really disliked Sparky, they just paid no attention to him. He never got up the nerve to ask a girl out. He knew he was a loser, and so did everyone else. At least that's what Sparky thought.

There was one thing that Sparky was good at, however; drawing. He especially liked to draw cartoons and actually worked up the courage to submit a few to his school newspaper. (They were promptly turned down.) Even after rejection Sparky decided to become a professional artist. He sent samples of his artwork to the Disney studios, but they too were sent back. Finally, Sparky decided to tell his own sad tale. He designed a series of cartoons around an underachieving, unappreciated boy who did not even get one card on Valentine's Day. Before long, the whole world knew the name of his cartoon counterpart, Charlie Brown.

It's a good thing Sparky, who we know as Charles Schulz, did not give up when he met with failure. How many of our lives, and those of our children and grandchildren, have been enriched because Charlie Brown's creator let his failures lead the way to success.

We are in great company, we members of Failures Anonymous. In fact, it's one of the largest groups in the world.

God Asks Women to Fail

We all want to be successful, however we define that. We encourage our children to succeed. We value success. It's way at the top of life's priority list. We regularly hear in most of our churches the good news of Jesus Christ as a positive, upbeat, esteem-generating, and self-worth-enhancing message. The gospel *is* positive, joyful, and wonderful, and we *are* highly valued by the Lord of all creation. In Isaiah 43:4 God tells us, "You are precious to me. You are honored, and I love you." However, God asks us to fail; to fall flat on our faces because it's good for us to come to the end of our resources, the end of ourselves, and to see ourselves for who we really are.

So why do we try so hard to cover up our failures, and our weaknesses? Well, we are not proud of them and should not be. Also, we sometimes try to cover our failings because we want to look good to other people and to God. Unfortunately, wanting to "perform" well tends to carry over to our spiritual self too. For most of us, instead of our just being willing to admit who we really are and to get real with the Lord and each other, we cover up. We hide. We pretend.

Sometimes we feel confident in our Christian life because we're checking off a list of do's or, more likely, don'ts, that we think lead to successful spirituality. When that checklist is comprised of external behaviors: what we wear, how we talk, what we listen to, what we do for religious "points," according to the tenets or traditions of our faith, we mistakenly feel that we are doing pretty well spiritually. Often, those around us who share the same external behavior lists will tend to agree that we are doing well.

Corrie Ten Boom shared her secret of maintaining a godly perception of her own worth, when others gave her accolades. She said that she thought of every compliment, each personal affirmation, every expression of praise and admiration she received as a beautiful rose. At the end of each day, Corrie said that she gathered up the roses, smelled them appreciatively and then handed the whole bouquet to the Lord, who alone is worthy of all praise.

Jesus frequently criticized the notion that keeping the externals of the law could make the secret heart of a person pure and acceptable to the holy God. Genuine faith, as Jesus described it, shows up in loving the Lord with all our heart, all our mind, and all our strength. Not only is that hard to monitor and evaluate, it is impossible to do. Think about the spiritually-related actions we *cannot* do—without Jesus Christ:

- We can't know God. (Romans 5:6–11)
- We can't approach God. (Romans 3:11)
- We can't obey God. (Galatians 3:22)
- We can't please God. (Galatians 2:19)
- We can't keep the law. (Galatians 2:21; 3:11)
- We can't have faith. (Ephesians 2:8–9)
- We can't do good. (Romans 3:10)

- We can't be forgiven. (Psalm 130:3–4; Romans 2:5; 5:6–11)
- We can't go to heaven. (John 14:6)
- We can't save ourselves. (Psalm 130:5; Ephesians 2:8–9)

We might as well admit it, we're not in very good shape. Secular society tells us to not be so down on ourselves; people are basically good, et cetera, et cetera. People *are* infinitely valuable, every single one of them; the unborn, the elderly, the obnoxious, and those different in mind and body from us. Everyone is priceless, but everyone is *not* basically good. Anyone who has observed a young child over time knows that none of us ever has to be "encouraged" toward misbehavior or a self-centered attitude or conduct. We're "naturals" at it.

However, just because we have all experienced failure, God does not want us to remain in "failure" mode. Recognizing our failures is a good thing, but continuing to focus on our lack of success is really a destructive focus on self, not a focus on God.

We have already recognized that the only focus worthy of our single-attention is the Lord Jesus Christ. A self-focus is something we want to remove from our lives, and staying stuck in failure-and-despair mode is actually a self-focus. A lingering, somber look at all our failings is also a lack of trust in what Jesus promises he can do to transform us to become someone useful, to bring glory to him and to help others. Our weakness is actually his most effective tool in using us for his glory and honor. So, how do we move from failure to success as seamlessly as possible?

God Wants Women to Succeed

My five-year-old grandson, Micah, recently had his first experience as a member of our church's littlest guys and gals' T-ball team, the Storm. I wouldn't miss a game because of my love for precious Micah, but also for the sheer entertainment of watching the America's-Funniest-Home-Videos-type chaos that was rampant during the first few competitive games.

Micah's fielding position was third baseman; where he stood, squatted, hunched over, and sat down, invariably facing the opposite direction from the batter at home plate, who was swinging and swatting at the ball in a futile attempt to make contact with it.

While "covering" third base, Micah tried to catch passing butterflies, traced the vapor trail of an overhead airplane with his finger, and drew in the dirt. Once or twice he even started to lie down, until he was spotted by the coach, his own daddy, and loudly admonished to "get up and pay attention!"

When occasionally a ball was actually hit by the fledgling batters, the entire fielding team could be seen vacating their various posts and leaving the infield completely bare in their joint attempt to retrieve the slowly rolling ball. One by one the tiny teammates tripped over each other as the ball crawled its way harmlessly through the infielders and out past the outfielders, while the amazed little batter ran around the bases for a victorious home run.

If a score had been kept, Team Storm's performance as a functioning T-ball team would have been ranked as an abysmal failure. No runs, few hits, all errors! But failure is only the "beginning" of the story. By the end of the short season, Micah's fellow Stormmates had evolved into a T-ball "machine" to behold. They could now catch and hit with an admirable degree of success, and when they ran from base to base they no longer zigzagged randomly from third to first to second to first again. The little T-ball champs even remembered to touch the bases they "conquered" as they ran past them, although raising a dark cloud of dirt as they skidded and slid around infield corners for dramatic impact was still a thrill they didn't want to give up.

It's important for us to recognize and remember that failure is an integral, inevitable part of the bigger picture called "success." Alexander Graham Bell made an accurate observation about the way we tend to look at failure in our lives. He said, rightly, "When one door closes, another opens, but we often look so long and so regretfully upon the closed door that we do not see the one which has opened for us." So true. We spend so much time regretting, wishing, "what if-ing," when actually Jesus wants to use us *today* and *for the rest of our lives,* no matter how many failures are in our past.

My husband and I got married and went to college together in Riverside, California, near my childhood home. Jim took a ceramics class one semester. It was the class most of the preacher boys took in lieu of the other options available at that hour, most of which were a little more academically challenging. It was a great social time for the young preachers to discuss how their weekend had gone at their churches, what they had preached on, and on and on.

After class one day, Jim took me to his vacant ceramics classroom to show me what he had made; a tall, but not too engineeringly-correct-in-its-design, umbrella holder. Sadly, it collapsed into itself. As we walked past his friend's teapot creation, Jim stopped and praised it, holding it up high by the curved handle for me to see. Unfortunately, the piece wasn't quite dry and the pot separated from the handle. Jim looked with horror as his friend's teapot crashed to the floor into a thousand pieces. There was no way that teapot would ever be able to be glued back together. I will never forget the look on Jim's face as he held the pot-less handle and then had to find his friend and confess what he had done. This mistake made me think of the passage in Jeremiah about the potter:

> This is the word that came to Jeremiah from the LORD "Go down to the potter's house, and there I will give you my message." So I went down to the potter's house, and I saw him working at the wheel. But the pot he was shaping from the clay was marred in his hands; so the potter formed it into another pot, shaping it as seemed best to him.
>
> (Jeremiah 18:1–4 NIV)

But God does not want us to remain in that sad condition. We are the reason he came to earth as Jesus; to seek and to save those who are lost, or misshapen, cracked, or squashed. When we come to the realization that we are an absolute failure without Jesus, we can take hold of his free gift of grace.

There is nothing we have ever done or ever will do that could possibly earn us our salvation. When we work to earn gifts, they aren't gifts anymore. They become pay, our entitlement, and we have already seen that we are entitled to none of God's favor. Ephesians 2:8–9 (NASB) explains that we cannot just try harder in order to be successful in our spiritual lives. "For by grace you have been saved through faith; and that not of yourselves, it is the gift of God; not as a result of works, so that no one may boast."

A magnificent iridescent dragonfly recently flew into our house through an open front door. Judging by his desperate efforts, the dragonfly must have been thinking, "If I just fly as hard as I can, with all my might and flying skill, toward that bright window in the ceiling, I'll be free." The entrapped insect did not understand that his open door to liberty stood only a few feet away, within easy flying range. He just tried harder and harder to extricate himself until all his strength was gone, battering and banging his wings against the skylight glass, and soon ending his life in total, futile exhaustion.

Trying hard is disastrously counter-productive. The majority of well-meaning people who depend upon their own goodness and righteous self-efforts to reach the heart of God, and the freedom from sin he offers, are tragically misguided and forever spiritually lifeless.

The number one criterion for getting fixed or repaired—no, remade completely, not just patched up—is to recognize our sins and failure, our need for saving, forgiving grace, and to humbly ask him for what he so freely gives. That's saving grace. And at that moment in time and eternity, we are changed instantaneously and forever from failures to beautiful trophies of success in God's gracious eyes. I believe that even after we have been changed from failure to success in God's eyes, our behavior lags behind the person we now are in reality, and we need God's strengthening grace to make us become who Jesus has designed and equipped us to be.

Many times, if we want to be useful to God, it is necessary for us to go through subsequent times of remolding by the Master Potter. He must sometimes repairs cracks we have acquired along the way or polish us up when we get dingy and dusty. Sometimes we are even placed into the kiln and things get hot. But God's continuing purpose for us is that we reach the point where we mirror his own reflection; a lifelong process.

The apostle Peter addresses the painful "repairs" that we must sometimes go through in our lives when he says:

> "In this you greatly rejoice, though now for a little while you may have had to suffer grief in all kinds of trials. These have come so that your faith—of greater worth than gold, which perishes even though refined by fire—may be proved genuine and may result in praise, glory and honor when Jesus Christ is revealed."
>
> (1 Peter 1: 6–7 NIV)

My children used to sing, "He's still working on me, to make me all I ought to be. He's still working on me." He is. Thank goodness, he is.

In our spiritual walk, failure equals success when we come to the end of ourselves and have exhausted our drive to live and do and be all we should for Jesus. Then at that crucial point, he takes over and energizes, restores, empowers, equips, and makes our efforts successful, as we allow him to.

I believe one of the most common tools God uses to bring us to the end of our inadequate resources, and the beginning of his limitless everything-we-need-for-life-and-godliness, is through irregular people in our lives, difficult circumstances, and demanding relationships. I remember seeing a friend in our church kneeling and crying brokenheartedly at the altar one Sunday morning, not because she had lost her job or was demoted, but because of a boss that was so difficult to work for.

In my case, I came to a point of painfully accurate self-analysis one day that I simply could not be everything I needed to be. I just did not have what it took to meet the demands at home, to be the absolutely "perfect" wife and mother that I wanted to be, to fulfill every vacant position in the church, and perform to everyone's expectation, especially my own.

I was painfully broken by my own lack of resources, my own inadequate performance, my own inability to do my number one job well, that of being a great wife and mother. I knew I was a failure, so I cried (literally), as I know you have too, over circumstances in my life. "Help, Lord. I can't do this," I told God. "I can't be nice enough, patient enough, affirming enough, cooperative enough, selfless enough to be all I should be for the people you've placed in my life. You'll have to live through me or I'll keep messing up again and again, and the job won't ever be done right."

I still don't do the job perfectly, but I know my ever-available source of grace, strength, wisdom, and love is Jesus, who is always ready and willing to live through me. He is everything that I am not.

Your failure may be in the area of getting along with a boss, a friend, a parent, a child, or dealing with a myriad of unique circumstances, but the journey to the end of ourselves is a great and necessary place for all of us to go. The process of letting go of our own resources sometimes hurts, but will never injure us. God wants to help us and then use us. If we could live the Christian life by ourselves, we wouldn't need Jesus, but how desperately we do need him. As we are avail-able, not able, Jesus himself becomes the *do-er* and *be-er* through our lives, our personality, our environment, and our opportunities.

Can you imagine a light bulb trying to shine without being connected to electrical energy? Picture a 75-watt bulb lying disconnected on the floor making every effort to shine. Or, imagine a puppet trying to perform with no hand inside it or a marionette with no one operating the strings. A car can't start itself and drive without a driver, can it? Nor can the Energizer Bunny keep on going without a battery. Jesus is our power source. When we are plugged into him, light is able to flow through us and bless everyone nearby. We are the broken and remade "teapot" he uses, as we let him, then, his efforts in and through us are absolutely successful. Praise his name!

My mother was a wonderful lady, full of energy and optimism. As a young teenager she absolutely loved life, and experienced it everyday with great enthusiasm. She had a zest for trying new things that one day got her in real trouble. My grandfather owned a family grocery store right on the corner of the tiny town square. There he made a living for Grandmother, my mother, and her nine brothers and sisters. Granddaddy worked as a farmer for his "other" job, and he would sell much of his fresh produce at the family's store in town. One day my mother's older brother needed to drive to town in the family's old pickup truck. Mother, always ready to go somewhere and do something, persuaded him to let her tag along in the passenger's seat; he reluctantly agreed. When they arrived in town, her brother parked the truck right in front of the big glass window at the front of the store that was my grandfather's pride and joy. My uncle ran into the store and took a little longer than he planned. As Mother sat in the old pickup in the heat of an Arkansas summer, she began to think of how much cooler it was when the truck was moving. With the side windows open, she loved the feel of the wind blowing through her hair.

In her typical, teenage, "I-am-invincible" thought process, my mother decided that it would really not be difficult to drive. She told herself, "I'll just drive around the square one time. No one will even know I'm gone. Then I'll pull right back into this same parking place."

No problem, except that Mother had never driven before. She was sure it must be as easy to drive as it looked. She managed to back the vehicle out of the parking space and aim it down the street, around the three corners in town and straight back toward the appointed position in front of the store. Miraculously, Mother actually circumvented the entire route without causing any calamities, that is, until the family truck hurtled right through the family store's plate glass window.

Thankfully, no one was hurt. The experience had a lasting effect on her whole life. For my mother, who remains forever in my heart as one of the most godly examples of a beautiful, controlled, committed, successful life, it was a painful illustration that she had the potential to act with less than perfect wisdom. Failure helped her to become all that she was.

I once heard a story about a young farm boy, who, like my mother, wanted to drive, not a truck, but his family's team of oxen. His daddy decided that it would be a good idea for the boy to learn how to handle the animals. The boy took the reins, wrapped them around his hands several times to make sure he had a firm grip and made the "clucking" sound that the oxen knew meant *go*. At first the pace was slow, much too slow for a boy on the verge of manhood with the power of the team in his hands, so he clucked again and the speed of the oxen increased, first to a trot, then to a run, then to an out-of-control gallop. The boy pulled and pulled on the reins, to no avail. Tears streamed down his cheeks and his heart seemed ready to beat out of his chest. He took a quick glance at his dad, who was just sitting there, watching the world go by. Finally, in total helplessness, the boy cried out to his father, "Daddy, I don't want to drive anymore."

We all need to come to the place where we say and mean it, "Lord, I don't want to drive anymore. Only you can turn my failure into success. Here I am; remake me and use me—for your glory."

A member of a delegation of visiting dignitaries once asked Mother Teresa if she ever grew discouraged because she had so few success stories in her life of sacrificial ministry. Her response was, "No, I don't get discouraged. God has not called me to a ministry of success. He has called me to a ministry of service and mercy."

A beautiful promise is found in 1 Chronicles 28: 20: "Be strong and courageous and do the work. Don't be afraid or discouraged by the size of the task, for the Lord God, my God, is with you. He will not fail you nor forsake you" (NIV).

Failures, missteps, broken promises, poor judgment calls, blatant sins, wrong turns, and broken storefront windows can be used as divine instruments to direct our focus to the One who creates beautiful, successful works of art from crushed vessels, cracked pots, chipped vases—and broken lives.

> Something beautiful,
> something good;
> All my confusion,
> He understood.
> All I had to offer Him
> was brokenness and strife—
> But He made something beautiful of my life.[3]

Chapter 3 Study Questions

1. Why do you think "success" is so highly regarded by society today?

2. What makes a person successful, according to popular secular opinion?

3. How does the Bible regard "failure"?

4. How do you think God defines "success"?

5. What role does failure play in true success?

6. All of us have failures in our lives that trouble us greatly and create guilt and regret. What do you believe God wants you to do with those sins, mistakes, and missteps that you've made in your life?

7. Satan is called, "the accuser of the brethren" (Revelation 12:10). How does he use his "power to accuse" in your life?

8. After we give our lives, failures and all, to Jesus Christ, how do you think he looks at all we've done, good and bad, past and present?

9. Think of three or four past or continuing failures that you wrestle with—that cause you grief and regret—and give them to God, who has completely erased every sin through his Saving Grace, and who will equip and enable you to be successful for him through his Strengthening Grace.

10. Think of three or four things that you do well or successfully that cause you to battle selfish pride, feelings of "I am really something!," superiority or self-sufficiency (different from the positive sense of accomplishment and gratitude that comes from a recognition that God has enabled you, gifted you, given you opportunities, etc. and they've gone well). Give those successes

to God, as well as your failures, thanking him for using you, and asking him to keep on doing so!

11. If you would like to do a personal study using this chapters topic, here are some Scriptures you may want to refer to:

Joshua 1:5
1 Chronicles 28:20
Psalm 71:5–8, 11–17
Isaiah 40:29–31
Luke 21:15–17; 22:31–34
2 Corinthians 12:10; 13:3–4
Philippians 3:12–14
Hebrews 11:33–34
Revelation 12:10

Proceed/Wait

Lisa

ave you ever been driving through town, say in the afternoon, with the sun beaming down, and you're listening to the radio with your mind on a zillion things, and you get to where you are going and you can't remember driving there?

Or scarier: You're in your car and you pass through an intersection and on the other side you say to yourself, "I hope that light I just went through was green or yellow, because I don't recall even seeing it."

Most modern-day women are preoccupied with so many things and moving so fast that many times we don't notice what is taking place around us.

I started thinking about how often I am completely oblivious to a simple thing like a traffic light because of all the things going on in my life; especially after having three children (I think I've been in a coma ever since). Although I am not convinced life can be summed up in one slogan, I am going to join the masses of self-appointed experts and coin my own phrase: Life is like a traffic light. I'll be more specific: The Christian life is like a traffic light.

A traffic light. What is its purpose? A traffic light signals what to do and when to do it. It gives drivers much needed instructions by beaming out a certain color and symbol. A traffic light is something that is so mundane and ordinary, yet it operates much like the Christian life. But here's the difference; instead of us being guided in our physical travels by an inanimate object operated by a computer somewhere; in the Christian life, we are guided by a very real and personal Holy God who actually gives us signals based upon each and every circumstance we face.

Does a traffic light care if you are late when it gives you a signal to stop? Believe me, I've asked this question many times, and for some reason I get no response! Does the traffic light let you go based on whether your destination is a good or bad place? If your credit card is maxed out and you are headed to the shopping mall, will the signal know that and change the light to stop you? Of course not. Because a traffic signal is not a feeling, thinking, discerning thing! But oh, how this differs from our Heavenly guide in our travels through life.

God Asks Women to Proceed

One of the hardest things God asks a woman to do is to proceed.

Women love the green lights of life. We have it all down to a science, don't we? We've got the angles figured out and the timing down pat, and we are rocking and rolling, zooming down the road of life. We love green, and we love to go. Going, in and of itself, is not necessarily bad. God created us with the capacity to "go" in life. He's told us directly in his Word, in certain instances, to go. Remember the Great Commission? "Go, ye, into all the world and preach the gospel" (Matthew 28:18–20 KJV).

But this is not what he is talking about when he asks women to proceed. *Proceed* is a much more deliberate word than *go*. While the word "go" immediately sends us off and on our way, without much thought involved, the word "proceed" causes us to give pause. Just listen to the deliberateness of these words that describe proceed: to advance, to continue, to ensue, to progress. Proceed is a much more deliberate word.

Proceed: Even Without All the Information

In 1993, my life was cruising along, hitting lots of green "go" lights. I had graduated from college six months prior and was working at my alma mater while waiting for my then-fiancé to finish up his last semester before we got married. Then after three years on "go," with my life moving along in a certain direction, I found myself at a red light. We broke up.

My dear mother, many miles away from me at the time, happened to call me on the night we ended our relationship. It was as if she sensed that I needed to hear from her. She was right. I was in a very fragile state. And even at the independent age of twenty-one, I still wanted the comfort of Mom. She suggested I come home for a week or so to clear my mind. Well, Mama always knows best, so I did just that.

I flew home to Missouri and took a break from my life. Why not? I was stuck at a traffic signal anyway. For days I lived in pajamas (which probably could have walked by themselves because they needed washing so badly). My hair needed serious attention, my red nose looked like Rudolph's, and my eyes were swollen and bloodshot. I was a mess!

Slowly, things began to get better. I revisited my standards of good hygiene and emerged from my cocoon-room. My family lived out in the country on some land, and I began to get outside more; the one place a real stoplight didn't exist. Pretty soon God started to do a work in me; I didn't know what the next step was, since the situation I had based all my decisions on no longer existed. My future was unsure. I did not have a lot of information to go on. But God was working. And I felt like he was telling me to proceed, in spite of my lack of direction.

Proceed on. But to do what? And where? And how? And why? See, for a logical and methodical thinker like me, these were very important questions that I felt I needed answered before I could make my move or take that next step. But God doesn't say that he is going to give us all the information all the time, does he? And I didn't have very much information to go on. But I knew in my spirit, and through prayer and seeking his face, that I needed to proceed. So I did just that.

Two months later I started graduate school in a different state, in a different part of the country. I did not know anyone or anything about the area, but I proceeded. God had a plan. I didn't know that in just a few short months I would meet my best girlfriend for life. I wasn't aware that this was where I would meet my life partner, my wonderful husband. He didn't fill me in on all the particulars. He just asked me to proceed. And I thank God that I did.

Many times the Lord is asking us to proceed in our lives, but we don't always have all the information, so many times we convince ourselves that this must mean that we shouldn't or can't move on with something. But that may be exactly how God wants it to be. He may want us to see what we will do without knowing all the details first. Know this, God doesn't leave anything out and he doesn't forget anything. He's purposeful with any and every omission of information. As it says in Psalm 145:13, 15 (NIV), "The Lord is faithful to all his promises and loving toward all he has made. . . . The eyes of all look to you, and you give them their food at the proper time." At the proper time. His timetable. He sets it, and he's never running behind.

We must realize that God is not required to appeal to our logic or our need for information; he doesn't owe us that or anything else. He doesn't have to fill us in, despite what we think! He reveals to us exactly what he wants to reveal when he wills it, and what he knows we can handle at that time. Oh sure, sometimes he lays it out for us in simple terms for us to understand; sometimes the direction is quite clear (and even then we don't always proceed). But sometimes it is his still small voice, his presence, and his spirit that bears witness with ours, that prompts us to proceed even when we don't know who, what, when, or even why.

Proceed: Even Without Knowing Why

My father told me that in Colorado, during the 1850s, an evangelist named Stephen Greleck had a deep desire to see the people in those majestic mountains come to know Christ. Every week he would ride up to a logging camp to preach the gospel to whoever would come and listen.

One day, Stephen felt that God was telling him to preach to the people at a logging camp that he had never been to before. So, without a question, he saddled up and set out for the camp. When he arrived there, he went inside what was the dining hall. It was empty. Not a soul was in sight. Stephen was puzzled; he bowed his head and started to pray. "Lord," he said, "I don't understand what I am doing here. You told me to come to this camp to preach, but there is no one to be found! Why am I here? What do you want me to do?" The Lord answered him and said, "Preach. Go ahead and preach, like I told you to."

Stephen wanted to be faithful to God and obedient to what he had asked him to do, so he opened up his Bible and began to preach like the place was full. He even gave an invitation at the end. He left the room and went outside, saddled up his horse, and went back down the hill.

Years later, Stephen Greleck was standing alone on London Bridge. A man approached him and asked, "Are you Stephen Greleck?" Stephen said he was. The man then said, "You don't know me, but years ago, I worked at a logging camp in Colorado. One Sunday morning, I found that I had forgotten to bring my axe home from work. So I went back to the camp to get it. When I got there, I heard a voice inside. I went up to the window and listened. You were preaching a sermon to an empty room as if hundreds were in attendance. You didn't know it, but I was listening to you from outside, and as I stood there listening God began to stir my heart. And when you gave an invitation, I bowed my head and asked Jesus Christ into my life. I became a Christian that day. I went back to work the next day and told two of my friends about what you said, and they too prayed to receive Christ. And now, all three of us are missionaries. We now preach the same gospel you did that day at the logging camp, where I was saved."

Even when Steven did not understand the "why," this servant of God was faithful to proceed as God had prompted him to. The results were enormous. The far-reaching impact of his action of obedience was multiplied in the lives of others for generations to come.

Like this country evangelist, we are to proceed on with things God instills in us, even without knowing what the end result will be. By not doing so, we risk missing the blessing he has for us and the privilege of serving him by doing his will.

Proceed: Even Despite Opposition

But there is another aspect to proceeding that we sometimes face. God does not assure us that we will not encounter obstacles or oppositions. He tells us in 2 Peter 3:3 that, "in the last days, scoffers will come, scoffing and following their own evil desires." Scoffers are people who will question you and cast doubt about what you are trying to do, so much so that they make you wonder if you are really even doing the right thing!

I heard this story once about Robert Fulton, the inventor of the steamboat. While I do not know the historical accuracy of it, it makes a strong point. As he was working on his seemingly endless project, his wife would stand at the stairs to the basement and watch him and say, "You'll never get it built. You can't do it." He continued on, and after many months of tedious work, finally one day he finished building it. So he called his wife downstairs and showed her his product. "Well, you may have gotten it built," she said, "but you'll never get it out of the house." Determined, he tore one of the walls of the basement out and got the contraption out of the house and on to the lawn. His wife came and saw what he had done and she said, "You may have gotten it on to the lawn, but you'll never get it down to the river."

So he got some mules and some logs and managed to get it down to the edge of the river. His wife saw this and said, "You may have gotten it to the river, but you'll never get it into the water without turning it over." So he maneuvered it down the riverbank into the river. And his wife looked and said, "Well, I'll tell you one thing. You won't ever get that thing to run. It'll never start." But Robert Fulton worked and worked until he finally got his invention started. And he took off down the river in his new steamboat. And as he did, he saw his wife running down the riverbank beside him, yelling over the loud roar of the machine, "You'll never get that thing to stop! It'll never stop!"

This funny picture of Robert Fulton's wife portrays a scoffer. She probably made him question what he was doing trying to build such an awesome contraption. He may have doubted himself and wondered why he had started this project in the first place. But he proceeded on, regardless of his wife's lack of support and outright ridicule. He was convinced that it would work, and he was willing to try.

I can't think of a more appropriate example of this in the Bible than the story of Noah and the ark from Genesis 6. Here we see that God is displeased with how corrupt and wicked the earth at that time had become. In verse 6 we are told, "The Lord was grieved that he had made man on the earth, and his heart was filled with pain." So out of his grief, he decided to wipe out all of mankind from the face of the earth by causing a great flood to sweep over everything and wash it all away.

Remember that Noah was a righteous man and "walked with God." So God told him how to survive this catastrophe. He instructed him how to build a massive boat and what to put in it. The last verse of chapter 6 says that Noah did just as God commanded him.

Can you imagine the ridicule Noah and his family endured? Day after day they hammered away while the people called him crazy, paranoid, silly, and worse. See, the people around him didn't have all the information; they didn't know God or his plan. Noah didn't let it bother him; he was convinced that what God said was true, and when the rains fell and the floods rose, at that moment, Noah, along with everyone else, had all the information right in front of him. I'm sure he was glad he had trusted God and proceeded on with what God had told him to do.

We must be convinced about our Lord and what he asks us to do. If he is asking you to proceed, then what you endeavor to do will work. His plans for you are not futile, and they always hold great purpose. Instead of building an invention like Robert Fulton, it may be something else. He may be prompting you to go on a mission trip, attend seminary, write a book, teach a Sunday school class, or minister to someone you just met. Whatever the case, you may have all the information you want, or you may not. But if God is prompting you to proceed, he has a reason in doing so.

Yellow Light: Proceeding with Caution

But just as a traffic light includes a red light and a green light, it also includes a yellow light. A yellow light literally means to "proceed with caution." While a green "go" light means drive without hesitation, a yellow light means to go ahead, but be cautious.

Such is the same for us as Christian women. It's as if God is saying, "Don't breeze through without giving it some thought. Be aware. Look to the left and to the right. Know what's going on around you." With yellow-light situations, even though we might have the right-of-way, we must be wise like Ecclesiastes 8:5 describes and use discernment and discretion.

God has given the Christian woman the tools and instruments to proceed in a responsible way. If you are waiting for someone in your life to tell you how and what and why and where, then you are looking for guidance in the wrong place. God's Holy Word will give you the guidance to know how to proceed and where to proceed, and maybe, even why to proceed.

When I read Philippians 3:12–14, it helps me to substitute "proceed" when Paul writes "press on" :

> Not that I have already obtained all this, or have already been made perfect, but I [proceed on] to take hold of that for which Christ Jesus took hold of me. Brothers [and sisters], I do not consider myself yet to have taken hold of it. But one thing I do: Forgetting what is behind and straining toward what is ahead, I [proceed on] toward the goal to win the prize for which God has called me heavenward in Christ Jesus (NIV).

Proceed on to win the prize. One of the hardest things God asks a woman to do is to proceed.

God Asks Women to Wait

I dare say that, for most of us, there's something much harder than being asked to proceed. Especially for a Type A person like me. Many times, God asks the Christian woman to wait.

If I were in a patience contest, I would never win first prize. See, I'm one of those people who, in line at the grocery store, jumps out of line to get in one that seems to be shorter. Don't you hate it when you move and then watch the original line move more quickly? The fact is that had you not been so impatient, you would have come out better. Waiting is hard to do, but it is also a huge part of life.

When you think about it, most of us spend an awful lot of time waiting on things. We wait at the hair salon when our stylist is running behind. We wait in line for the bathroom at church or at a restaurant or an event. We wait in traffic. We wait for long periods of time to get on a ride at crowded amusement parks. We wait for doctor appointments and at fast food windows and at the movies. We teach our kids from the time they are born that they need to wait on things because we have learned to value this principle, and we know what a hard time people have grasping it.

Some of the shortest books in the Old Testament hold the richest truths about waiting. Listen to what it says in Lamentations 3:25–26 (NIV), "The Lord is good to those whose hope is in him, to the one who seeks him; it is good to wait quietly for the salvation of the Lord." Habakkuk 2:3 says, "For the revelation awaits an appointed time; . . . it will not prove false." Hosea 12:6 says, "But you must return to your God, maintain love and justice, and wait for your God always."

God asks a woman to wait, but how should we wait when we really want to "go"? I think there are some important ways in which we should wait on God.

Wait with Integrity: The Spilled Pennies Story

Scott and I had been dating for about six months. We had gotten pretty serious about each other, and I felt sure he was going to ask me to marry him sometime in the near future. As a matter of fact, I had a hunch that he had a ring in his apartment for me. So one afternoon, when he was in class, I stopped by his apartment before going to work. On the drive over I had talked myself into thinking that I really needed to find the hidden ring and see it for myself. I justified this by telling myself that I needed to make sure I liked it so I wouldn't look horrified when he gave it to me if I didn't. And after all, I thought to myself, I don't like surprises.

At his apartment I had only a few minutes to spare, so I went to the old faithful spot under the bed. No dice. I looked in the bedside table, too obvious. I rummaged through his chest of drawers, not there. I resorted to looking in his underwear drawer and under the mattress. Still no ring. So, out of time, I decided to give up. On my way out I passed his laundry room and noticed a medium-sized brown box on the shelf above the washer and dryer. Aha! I thought to myself. So, in my work uniform, with my high heels on, I hoisted myself up onto the top of the dryer. As I did, I remembered that Scott told me that he liked to dump his loose change in a cup in the laundry room, and I noticed too late a large plastic cup next to the box. My reaction time could not catch up with my thoughts, and my hand was not as quick as my eye. To my horror, the large cup fell to the ground. It was like watching a scene in slow motion. I saw myself yelling "Noooooooooooooo" as the cup hit the floor and sent hundreds and hundreds of pennies between and behind and under the washer and dryer. The evidence of my impatience, so to speak, was everywhere.

I learned a great lesson that day. Romans 8:25 says that, "if we hope for what we do not yet have, we wait for it patiently." I had the hoping-for-what-I-did-not-yet-have part down, but I struck out on the wait-for-it-patiently part. I was so impatient to see that ring that I took matters into my own hands (or tried to!) and the result was a mess. (Luckily, Scott forgave me and asked me to marry him anyway. The ring *was* in the apartment; think filing cabinet.)

We need to not only wait on God, but also to wait on him with integrity. Sometimes we get impatient and take matters into our own hands, and in the process, we make a huge mess. We spill the pennies, things fall out of our grasp and come crashing down, and the evidence is all around us. We try our best to clean up, but sometimes it's too far gone and we can't get it all. We try to cover it up so God won't see the results of our impatience, but he does. He sees. He knows. He knows it when we have that first thought of, "I'm tired of waiting on this. I'll just do a little something on my own. Surely that can't hurt." We want our agenda, our way, our timing, but we need to wait with integrity.

Sadly, none of us are really very good at waiting, are we? We live in a hurry-up world. Banks, food chains, shopping malls, even churches cater to our "here and now" mentality. The five-minute lunch. The two-minute deposit. Curb service.

Do you remember the story of Job in the Bible? After his family, possessions, and health had been taken away, Job waited, and waited, and waited on God. Then he waited some more. Even his wife turned against him and tried to get him to turn against God. Listen to the words she used in Job 2:9: "Are you still holding on to your integrity? Curse God and die!" Nevertheless, Job waited on God with integrity, and everyone who saw him witnessed it. Job himself sums it up in verse 14 of chapter 14, "If a man dies, will he live again? All the days of my hard service I will wait for my renewal to come." Psalm 25:21 says this, "May integrity and uprightness protect me, because my hope is in you." Wait on God with integrity.

Wait with Expectation: Swollen Ankles, Tired Feet

Some of you know the drill. Calculate. Estimate. Mark the calendar. Check the calendar. Determine the date. Set the mood. Accomplish the task. Wait. Estimate again. Buy the white box. Take the test. And wait. Get the good news. Make the appointment. Then wait. Get impatient. Take another test. Get the good news again. Then wait. Go to your appointment. Get the good news again. Then wait. And keep waiting and waiting and waiting and waiting. Mothers-to-be play possibly the longest waiting game of a woman's life. Yes, the privilege of having children is such a joy; I have three blessings of my own. But the pregnancy part—not so much joy.

From start to finish, a pregnant woman waits an excruciating amount of time to finally reach that pinnacle of delivery. And at that point, she has so become this other creature with red eyes, disfigured belly, and swollen feet that she would be willing to have anyone—the UPS driver, the soccer coach, anyone—deliver the baby just so she can get it out. For those of you who have not yet borne a child, rest assured that pregnancy and childbirth are truly amazing miracles of God, but this is not a short process. It's a process that involves a lot of waiting.

There's an element within the waiting, though, that helps make it bearable, perhaps even exciting. Expectation. Galatians 5:5 (NIV) says, "But by faith we eagerly await through the Spirit the righteousness for which we hope." No matter what you're waiting for, you too should be waiting *expectantly.*

God wants to do an amazing work in our life, but not this instant. It's not like the oatmeal packets that we pop into the microwave for a hot breakfast in two minutes. As we wait for whatever he has for us, we must be expecting great things. There is no room for gloom-and-doom in the Christian life; not because the world is full of good, or we are so capable of living a great life, but because God is good—and capable. He is in control of our life because we asked him to be. We should expect nothing less than what God Almighty is capable of giving, and that is the very best. Remember James 1:17, "Every good and perfect gift is from above, coming down from the Father of the heavenly lights, who does not change like shifting shadows" (NIV).

Hannah is a good example of one who waits expectantly on the Lord. She was an older woman who desperately wanted to have a child. While many women would have given up after such a long time, Hannah waited with an expectation that God would give her a baby. She prayed to the Lord to grant her this deep desire of her heart; she waited, she prayed some more, and she waited with the great longing of becoming a mother. Then, 1 Samuel 1 says that "God remembered her." So after all the tears and the prayers and the waiting, he gave her a son named Samuel.

But it wasn't just an old married woman who waited with expectation. Two of the most famous single girls in the Bible were involved in a fascinating story about waiting. Rachel, the younger, was known for her desirability, while Leah, the eldest, was known for her "good personality." Jacob wanted Rachel as his wife, but unfortunately in those days the older sister had to be married first. Through an agreement with the girls' father, Jacob labored for seven years to earn the hand of his beloved Rachel. But on the first morning of his honeymoon, he discovered that he had been deceived; his new bride was Leah. He would not give up, though. He worked another seven years for Rachel. Talk about waiting with expectation!

Wait with Resolution: Bound and Determined

A young girl named Jann Mitchell grew up in a small Southern California town with a big dream. She didn't know how, she didn't know when, but she was bound and determined to accomplish her dream.

Every week Jann would go to her neighborhood's yellow library with brown trim to get new adventure books to read at night. One day, as the white-haired librarian was stamping her selections for the week, the little girl wondered aloud at what it would feel like to have a book of one's own displayed at the library for all to see. Solemnly she confessed her secret dream: "When I grow up, I'm going to be a writer; I'm going to write books."

The librarian smiled, not with condescension, but with encouragement. "When you do write that book," she replied, "bring it into our library and we'll put it on display, right here on the counter."

Jann never let go of her determination to be a writer. She got her first job in ninth grade, writing personality profiles for a dollar fifty a piece. A few years later, she became the editor for her high school newspaper. She married and started a family, but the itch to write burned deep. She got a part-time job at a weekly newspaper writing columns. It kept her brain busy as she balanced babies. She went to work full-time for a major daily and also tried her hand at magazines. No book yet, but she still dreamed.

Finally, she believed she had something to say and completed a manuscript. She sent it off to two publishers and was rejected. Even though she put it aside for a time, she kept on dreaming. Several years later, the old dream increased in persistence. So she wrote another book. She pulled the other out of hiding, and soon both were sold. For two long years, she waited for her books to be published.

On the day that the box arrived on her doorstep with its author's copies, she ripped it open and cried. Then she remembered the librarian's invitation, and her promise. The librarian had since died, but she wrote the new one and asked if she could bring by her books to donate to the library when she was in town for her thirtieth high school reunion. The librarian agreed.

Jann found the big bright new library right across the street from her old high school, nearly on top of the spot where her old house had stood. Inside, she presented the books to the librarian, who placed them on the counter with a sign of explanation. Outside, Jann Mitchell, current author and once 10-year old dreamer, posed by the library sign next to a board with the words, *Welcome Back, Jann Mitchell.*[4]

Many of us are like Jann Mitchell. We have a dream, a goal, a desire or a request that we want God to fulfill in our lives, and after waiting for a period of time, sometimes a long period, we wonder if it's ever really going to happen. We wonder if God is going to answer our prayers at all.

But God asks a woman to wait with resolution. With great resolve, trust, hope, and faith, we must wait with steadfast confidence in our Lord, and believe that he will do what he says he will do in our lives. Psalm 27:14 reminds us to "wait for the Lord; be strong and take heart and wait for the Lord." Be strong and be resolved, while waiting on God.

Waiting Builds Character

Is eighteen months a long period of time or a short period of time? It depends on what you are talking about, right? If I were to tell you that you had eighteen months to live, you would probably say that that is much too short. But what about if you had to go to prison for eighteen months? In that situation, it would feel like an eternity.

In 2002, our life came to a red light when my husband lost his job. We were devastated by the news, especially since we were four weeks away from having our third child, but we were initially optimistic that God wouldn't keep us in that state for long. After all, we rationalized, my husband had both a college and graduate degree, and he was smart, capable, and hard working. We were sure that this was simply a temporary set-back for us, but oh, how wrong we were. Two weeks went by, and then two months, four months, eight months, a year and all the way to eighteen months. God had us in a holding pattern for a year and a half. Can I tell you that it was not okay with me? It was really inconvenient for me to have to wait for so long. It was a struggle to remain positive and keep our faith strong. We were in an eighteen-month valley, and at times it seemed like we were going to be in *wait* mode permanently.

One of the most difficult aspects of this was that my husband and I both happen to be go-getters; we are both motivated people who like to *do it* and *do it now*. So being the non-waiters that we are, we assumed that God would sense this. Surely he would know that we couldn't handle it if it dragged on and on, and in our feeble minds we surmised that we were ready to move on and see what the next thing he had for us was. We felt that our hearts were in the right place, now *he* just needed to hurry up and get on with it!

To be sure, the silence from God in this wait mode was almost deafening. It literally seemed like the clocks were ticking slower and slower and the days were getting longer and longer as we stood by helplessly with straightjackets on and gags in our mouth. At first it was very uncomfortable. We struggled a lot. We became increasingly cynical and overwhelmingly introverted. We read many self-help books and inspirational stories with encouraging titles, as we grasped to figure out the why and when and who and how. We knew God loved us, so why was he doing this to us? But you know what happened after six, eight, twelve, fifteen weeks of this? It started getting a little easier and a little less heavy and a little more comfortable. Why? Were the days getting shorter and the clocks ticking faster? No. But we had begun looking at the calendar and the clock less often, because we realized that we had to let go of everything, stop rushing God, and submit to the waiting process. We began to wait with the resolution that God had it all worked out, and it wasn't bothering him a bit to wait a while to fulfill his purpose in us. It had nothing to do with a calendar on the wall; we soon came to figure out that calendars are man-made, not God made.

You're probably familiar with the well-known passage from Philippians where it says "Do not be anxious for anything, but in everything, by prayer and petition, with thanksgiving, present your requests to God. And the peace of God, which transcends all understanding, will guard your hearts and your minds in Christ Jesus" (Philippians 4:6–7 NIV). In the same chapter a little further on (verses 11–13), Paul gives us a very important example; he lets us in on a life secret: "I have learned to be content whatever the circumstances. I know what it is to be in need, and I know what it is to have plenty. I have learned the secret of being content in any and every situation, whether well fed or hungry, whether living in plenty or in want. I can do all things through him who gives me strength."

Here is our goal: to be content no matter what the scenario or circumstance. Yet we must not be deceived into believing that this can be accomplished in our own strength. Waiting can only be achieved with the help of our Lord Jesus Christ, because waiting is one of the hardest things God asks a woman to do.

I read a story once about a farmer and his son who farmed a little piece of land in a quiet village. Several times a year they would load up their old cart with vegetables and go to the nearest city to sell their produce. Except for their name and the joint piece of land they farmed together, they had little in common. The old man believed in taking it easy; the boy was usually in a hurry. One morning they hitched up the ox to the loaded cart and started on the long journey. Of course the son wanted to walk fast, traveling day and night to make it to the market by early the next morning, but the father felt differently about it. He wanted to take his time, to see his brother along the way, to stop and smell the roses.

The day came and went, with the son feeling irritated and the father feeling tired. They found a place to stop and sleep. Before sunrise the young man shook his father awake, and they hitched up and started out. A few miles down the road they ran into another farmer, a stranger, trying to pull his cart out of a ditch. The father wanted to help the man, but his son wanted to keep moving; eventually age won out. Just about the time they finished pulling the man's cart out of the ditch, a great flash split the sky followed by what sounded like thunder. The sky grew dark and smoky. It was late in the afternoon when they reached the hill overlooking the city. They stared down at it for a long, long time. Neither of them said a word. They turned their cart around and began to roll slowly away from what had once been the city of Hiroshima.[5]

We can learn a great truth from this story. Had the man and his son gotten to the village any sooner, they would have perished in this horrific event. As they traveled along, they couldn't see what was ahead, they could only react to what they were facing on their journey. In the same way, we must trust that when God asks us to wait, he knows what he is doing. Only he knows what is ahead for us.

"But they that wait upon the LORD shall renew their strength; they shall mount up with wings as eagles; they shall run, and not be weary; and they shall walk, and not faint" (Isaiah 40:31 KJV).

Chapter 4 Study Questions

1. Spend some time this week searching your heart to see if there are things in your life God is asking you to proceed with. Ask the Lord to provide you with the insight and wisdom to determine when to proceed and how to proceed.

2. Examine obstacles that might be in the way of your proceeding with something. Identify them and give them over to God, asking him to provide you with the strength and trust in him that you need to overcome them.

3. Determine what you believe your patience level generally is in most areas of life: (On a scale of 1–10: 1-not very patient; 10-very patient). Submit yourself to the scrutiny of the Holy Spirit and ask him to show you the areas of your life where you should be more patient. Ask him to give you peace and faith to rest in him.

4. Search your heart to see if you are waiting on God with integrity, or taking matters into your own hands. Are you waiting with a positive attitude towards God and expecting great things from him for your life? Ask the Lord to give you more resolve to wait on him as he fulfills his will for your life. Thank him for his patience with you.

5. If you would like to do a personal study using this chapter's topic, here are some Scriptures you may want to refer to:

Proceed	*Wait*
Genesis 6–9	2 Kings 6:33
Matthew 28:18–20	Job 14:14
Psalm 145:15	Psalm 25:3, 5, 21; 37:9, 34; 52:9;
2 Peter 3:3	59:9; 62:5; 69:3, 6; 123:2
Philippians 3:12–14	Proverbs 20:22
	Isaiah 8:17; 30:18; 40:31; 59:9
	Jeremiah 14:22
	Lamentations 3:25
	Hosea 12:6
	Micah 7:7
	Habakkuk 2:3
	Zephaniah 3:8
	Luke 12:36
	Acts 1:4
	Romans 8:25
	Galatians 5:5
	1 Thessalonians 1:10

Hold On/Let Go

Kathie

I have always wanted to be athletic. It looked like so much fun. (If walking on a treadmill is a sport, I'm okay at that one.) I have made two memorable attempts at participating in a sport. I'll just say that the best part was the lessons I learned about holding on and letting go.

A number of years ago we lived at Lake Elsinore in Southern California where my husband served as pastor of a local church. He kept trying to persuade me to water-ski. I'm not a great swimmer and didn't consider learning to stand up on skis behind a rapidly moving boat a cause worth risking my life for. He promised he would drive the boat at the perfect speed and pick me up immediately if I fell. I reluctantly gave in.

I tightened my life jacket, slid into the water, adjusted the wobbly skis, and steeled my resolve for take off. My loving husband's final instructions were, "If you fall, let go of the rope." He cranked up the boat, and slowly, awkwardly, sort of like the apostle Peter, I found myself actually standing on the water. Amazing. That lasted for about a second and a half. Down I went, and I immediately forgot Jim's admonition to let go of the rope. The boat *and I* both circled around and around trying to pick me up. Unfortunately, I couldn't hear Jim crying, "Let go of the rope." because I was too busy swallowing Lake Elsinore.

My second attempt at athletics involved the winter counterpart: snow skiing. I mounted the chairlift with one of my children while the other child and my husband followed in the chair behind us for moral support. (Like it would realistically do any good if something happened while on the lift.) It only took a matter of seconds for me to realize in horror that the lift only took passengers *up*, and that to get down the mountain by any means other than upright on skis meant I would have to be seriously injured on a stretcher. Yes, I considered that for a moment. Then rationality returned, but not before I identified with my children's movie, *Snowball Express*, and began to evaluate my options for saving the neck I valued greatly. I watched my children wave (for what I was sure was our final goodbye) as they passed me, swerving effortlessly from side to side. Had we been in the same bunny-slope class? They obviously had already learned to let go and let fly.

As I inevitably picked up momentum on the way down "Sure and Sudden Death Mountain" (my new name for it), my unwise tack was to face my knees inward, throwing myself into an immediate out-of-control skid and tumble. Getting up was a slippery challenge, with my skis acting like giant spears, tossing me about like a stuffed animal. A gracious stranger on her own trip downhill noticed my plight and patiently encouraged me to "let go" sufficiently to get to the bottom of the mountain. I still consider her my personal skiing angel.

I've decided that for me, holding on comes more easily than letting go. We all have to learn to do both, and at the appropriate time.

A toddler will reach into a small-mouth jar to get a piece of candy inside, and then get stuck when the treasure in his fist makes it impossible to pull it out of the jar. In fact, little ones will pick up almost anything: a razor blade, a knife, a lighted match, a bee, a snake. When my sister's oldest boy was a toddler, the family lived in Southern California on the edge of the desert in a town appropriately known as Sunland. One summer day my sister saw her little boy bend down to pick up something he found interesting; a furry, brown tarantula.

Remember Aesop's fables? There was one story about a dog crossing a bridge with a bone in his mouth. He noticed his reflection in the river below and wanted that "other" bone too. The greedy animal dropped the real bone to grab the reflection, losing the delicious thing in the process.

We can see ourselves in my little nephew or the not-so-bright dog on the bridge, can't we? So often we hold on to things that don't deserve our grasp and let go of, or carelessly and loosely hold onto, the real things that have tremendous eternal value.

What Does God Ask Us To Let Go Of?

Peter had to let go of the safety and security of his fishing boat to come to Jesus. Perhaps you've been in a similar situation. You made a difficult move, letting go of everyone and everything that represented home and security to you; then you entered a dark and troubling time like the threatening waters that terrified Peter.

Jesus told his disciples to let go of most of their earthly possessions and to spread the gospel with little more than the clothes on their backs. He told them, and us, to let go of anything that can be used as an excuse for not following him or that causes us to have a dual allegiance, a double-mind, a divided loyalty—even if it's a new wife, the need to bury a parent, or a hand or eye that gets us into trouble.

That sounds so extreme. Would it really hurt to hold onto those prior commitments? Jesus is Lord, and true love and obedience to him requires 100 percent of our loyalty and service. Is there anything wrong with a husband expecting 100 percent of his wife's devotion and faithful love and not being willing to settle for 80 or 90 percent? Much more so, Jesus wants us to let go of anything that encumbers us and slows us down in our spiritual journey, not like a runner with ankle weights, holding onto barbells, wearing heavy clothing.

One: Let Go of Fear

Imagine yourself in a boxing-match with Satan. You may find yourself wanting to grab hold of the ropes around the perimeter, but that only makes you a better target. If you stop moving and hold on to the ropes, you'll get pummeled until you can't stand up. Fear is one of the ropes I find myself grasping tightly. Fear causes us to cling to something that will hurt us, not help us.

When I was in high school, many years ago, I went out with an upper classman who loved speed. I loved safety. He picked me up in his iridescent blue car that he had literally built himself —and that he loved more than life itself. It was obvious he was convinced he was going to impress me with the thrill ride of my life, but from that point on I felt only stark terror. I have no idea where we went because my eyes were welded shut and my knuckles were white from holding onto the pipe in front of me that served as a dashboard.

Sometimes fear isn't quite so dramatic. It can show up in our lives in a variety of ways:

Fear leads to worry. Worry is turning over and over in our mind all the "what if" scenarios we can imagine, until they become as real to us as actual "Oh, no" events. What does God tell us about worrying? Let go of it. "Don't worry about anything; instead, pray about everything. Tell God what you need, and thank him for all he has done" (Philippians 4:6). What positive good does worrying do? Nothing. Worrying is a rope we hold onto that only hurts us and undermines our trust in God, who can handle everything we now face or ever will face.

Ruth Graham tells how fear and worry stalked her nights because of her overwhelming concern for a child whom she loved so much—until one night when she opened her Bible to 2 Thessalonians for solace: "Be anxious for nothing, but in everything by prayer and supplication with thanksgiving, let your requests be made known unto God." In her mother's heart, she began to thank God for her beloved child, his gifts, his life, the plans God has designed for him, and the peace of God began to guard her heart and mind, and to give her rest. God's great plans were accomplished in the life of her child.

Fear keeps us in our comfort zone. That doesn't sound so bad, does it? What's wrong with comfort? But comfort is very closely linked with complacency and mediocrity. We become satisfied and content with low goals and easy expectations for ourselves.

Fear makes us not want to get out on a limb at all, or not very far. But God wants us to make ourselves available to do whatever he has in mind for our lives. The Lord's wonderful plan for our lives includes stretching us to take us to the next level, where we can see panoramic spiritual sights we would have otherwise completely missed.

If we are afraid, we may hold back from God and put our brakes on, like I did when I was trying to ski. He wants us to say, "Here I am, Lord, use me." But we often want to hear what he has in mind before we commit to something we think might be uncomfortable for us.

Moses was afraid when God called him, his mind and heart were filled with feelings of inadequacy and insecurity, but the Lord had all the bases covered for Moses. He was going to use his talents, and lack of them, to the fullest. God's plans for Moses were amazing, as this man of God, with feet of clay, would learn time after time. Moses would learn to fully trust God—fear and worry were futile, worthless, counterproductive emotional exercises.

Fear sometimes makes us a controller. We are afraid not to micromanage the details of our life, instead of resting in Jesus and letting him manage them for us.

Fear sometimes creates a lack of honesty, a lack of openness and candidness because we feel we need to protect ourselves from what others might think of us if we opened up and let people really know who God made us to be.

We need to let go of our fears, and learn to give them to Jesus. We may experience the emotion of fear—I do when I fly in an airplane, but I choose to trust God and fly. I feel fear when I try to share the good news of Jesus Christ, but my emotions are irrelevant, I'm commissioned to tell others about Jesus, in spite of how I feel at the time. The psalmist tells us, "The LORD is with me; I will not be afraid. What can man do to me?" (Psalm 118:6 NIV), and Jesus tells us, "Peace I leave with you; my peace I give you. I do not give to you as the world gives. Do not let your hearts be troubled and do not be afraid" (John 14:27 NIV).

Two: Let Go of Hurt

A newspaper cartoon showed a badly injured man lying on his living room couch while in the next room his wife dutifully shuffled through hospital bills and insurance forms regarding his accident. As the poor man lies there, leg and arm in traction, bandaged from head to toe with only his eyes and mouth visible, his wife slices her finger on a piece of paper and screams "Ouch, there's nothing worse than a paper cut."

No doubt physical pain can be miserable. However, it is often not the worst kind of pain. How often have we experienced emotional, psychological, mental, or spiritual trauma? Hurt, like fear, has basic elements that are usually present:

Disappointment. Hurt is often delivered by someone we loved, trusted, looked up to, placed our hope in—and that very person,

108

or that circumstance we counted on—turned on us and caused us great pain.

Disillusionment, tied to disappointment. We thought that things would turn out differently; that an accusation or innuendo against someone we respected would prove untrue, that our prayers would be quickly answered in a specific way and they were not, that someone we put on a pedestal as a terrific Christian let us down, and the pain we feel is real, and is sometimes directed toward God himself.

Unfairness. Justice is an element present in practically every hurtful situation in our lives. Perhaps unfairness is allowed to be there so that we will have to extend forgiveness at some point, even when we're not at fault, and often, without an apology from those who inflicted the pain. Jesus was our example of One who endured total unfairness. He deserved nothing that he experienced for our salvation and our forgiveness. All that we can do is follow his example and allow him to enable us to let hurt go.

Anger. This is a normal part of hurt and grief and loss. If what we experience is not actual anger, it may be a sense of frustration because we cannot change the situation we are in—or we cannot find resolution and closure. Hurt so often does not come in a neat little package, with apologies and hugs and sweet fellowship forever after, because there is, inevitably, more than one person involved, and each is making choices. Our anger arises because of the unfairness, the disappointment, and the inability to do anything about it.

I got a call that a good friend of mine had died of an aneurysm that no one knew she had until it was too late. She left behind a husband and one precious daughter. There are likely going to be frustrating questions and hurt feelings on her daughter's part: "Why did this have to happen?" "Why didn't I get to have her here longer?" "I need her." Some of you have been where this young lady is.

Anger is a normal part of the hurting and healing process and doesn't mean we don't love God. But the continuing, smoldering, bitter kind of anger that stays and slowly burns and grows, that paralyzes our life and usefulness, can one day fill our heart and choke the joy, the peace, and the productive life out of us. At some point, we must let go of anger. It may take time and Jesus will help us.

Fear. Yes, fear is often a part of hurt. It makes us not want to be vulnerable; to love, to commit, to give of ourselves again for fear we'll experience more hurt. So we give mixed signals to people—come close, stay away, come close, stay away. Or we climb inside a protective emotional bubble so people cannot reach us. We live with an invisible spray-on Band-Aid on our heart so that no hurt can reach us, but in doing so, the love and compassion of Jesus Christ can't get out.

An opportunity for real growth and service. We all know people who have turned their own personal, irreplaceable loss and hurt into healing for themselves and service to other people.

My friend Richard helps and serves other people in very practical ways because he took care of two younger brothers who contracted muscular dystrophy and died in childhood. Richard developed a spirit that desires to serve.

Mary, a single mom, turned her experience of overwhelming betrayal into tremendous credibility, empathy, and compassion, extended to the girls and women who come into her home beauty shop each day.

Beth Ann, an unmarried college student, became pregnant and made adoption possible for a family who desperately wanted a baby. Beth Ann and her family are now using their difficult personal journey as a practical help, inspiration, and encouragement to other women and their families.

Our journeys are different, but to all of us, Jesus says, "Cast your burdens and cares upon me—and I will sustain you"—a promise from the one who cannot lie. To "cast" means we have to let go and, like so many other verses in the Bible, this one is very likely a continuing action verb, not just a one-time-will-do-it word. It means that we will probably need to "keep on" placing our heavy burden and our deep pain on Jesus, over and over again. Finally we come to the place where we understand that he wants to carry all our hurt and all our pain. What a precious Savior and friend.

Three: Let Go of Expectations

We may see a child getting excited over a brightly wrapped present. She is sure something wonderful is inside—a new puppy, or a toy she's been dreaming of. But then we see disappointment on the child's face when what is inside the package doesn't measure up to her expectations. Maybe the parent tries to smooth things over, with a comment like, "Isn't that nice, honey? Tell Mrs. Jones thank you." The child's somber compliance only verifies her crushed expectations. Children aren't too good at covering up their feelings. Maybe adults aren't, either, and life is sometimes not what we expected. We're childlike in our expectations of God; we're just sure he'll make things happen as we picture them:

We'll get that raise we have been working toward.

A new job will open up, right after we lose ours.

The doctor's report will be good.

Our child will get the teacher we prayed for.

Our friends, who are having marital problems, will get them worked out.

Our tax refund will be big enough to pay for that trip.

But, what if those things don't happen? Sometimes what we think are the obvious "best" choices for our lives don't occur.

Dwight L. Moody, the great nineteenth-century preacher, once said "Character is who we are in the dark." Yet, much of the time, when our urgent expectations are not met and we feel completely in the dark about what God is doing, we are less concerned about our character than about getting what we want.

Jesus talked about expectations in Luke 11:11–12, when he said, "Which of you fathers, if your son asks for a fish, will give him a snake instead? Or if he asks for an egg, will give him a scorpion?" Of course not. They expect something good from us. Likewise, we can count on knowing that whatever our Heavenly Father gives us (whether we like it, understand it, or agree with it), will be *good*. What do we "expect" God to do for us as his children? We expect that he will provide a smooth, easy life if we serve him faithfully and support his church financially. We expect him to respond "in kind"—to allow us financial prosperity, or at least no job loss. We expect that he will keep us healthy and happy for our whole life, day in and day out. We expect committed believers to never experience depression or disappointment, after all, we're Christians. Christians don't get gloomy.

We need to let go of false expectations of how and when God will work. As we fervently, earnestly, confidently ask for what we want and need (as he tells us to do) we need to approach him with a heart of submission. Think of Jesus in the Garden of Gethsemane when he said "Abba, Father, everything is possible for you. Please take this cup of suffering away from me. Yet I want your will to be done, not mine." We must allow the Lord of all to be the Lord of all in our lives. "Trust in the Lord with all your heart, and lean not on your own understanding. In all your ways acknowledge him and he shall direct your paths" (Proverbs 3:5–6 NKJV).

Four: Let Go of Control

I have a love/hate relationship with airplanes. I love the convenience and time saved by flying to visit my family in California, the Midwest, and New Hampshire. I enjoy looking out on God's beautiful sky as the plane reaches altitude above the weather below, but I hate the feeling of having "nothing" under my feet. I especially don't like the out-of-my-control, no-turning-back-now feeling I get during takeoff. I guess I like to be in charge, and when it comes to piloting a plane, I'm not at all qualified.

A few months ago I was on my way to visit my son and daughter-in-law and their two little boys in Derry, New Hampshire. As I sat in the small jet awaiting takeoff, I performed my usual before-flight ritual of fastening my seat belt, adjusting my air vent, and praying. Our turn for takeoff came, so we headed down the runway and began to pick up speed. Faster, faster, higher, and higher whined the engines, the nose of the plane was on the verge of lifting up, when suddenly, *WHEEOOOoooo*, everything shut down. I sat motionless as the pilot's voice came over the intercom explaining that a red warning light had flashed in the cockpit of the small plane and that he had aborted takeoff.

We sat on the plane for several hours while mechanics and airport personnel worked to find the problem and fix it. I felt as if I had no control over my own life and safety. I had been instructed not to change planes; I didn't know what the problem was or if it could be fixed. I just knew that I was going to fly on that broken plane at some point, and that I was under the control of those in charge of making all the decisions.

Actually, that was okay. Why? Because I knew the One who was *really* in charge of our limping plane. I could trust God even if I didn't have all the other information I wanted. (The plane was eventually repaired, we took off successfully, and I had a great visit.) The situation had been under control all the time; just not my control.

Often our human tendency is to want to be in control of our lives and especially specific circumstances, but many times events that occur are simply out of our control. That does not feel good to us. Psalm 18:2 and 61:3 both describe God as our "tower"; our high tower, our strong tower. We like the idea of him being our Protector, our Defender, we just don't especially want him to be our control tower, in spite of the fact that at some point in our past we asked him to be our Lord.

When I looked in the concordance there were twenty-four pages containing the word *lord*; some of the verses say:

"I am the Lord; I change not."

(Malachi 3:6 NKJV)

"You shall worship the Lord and only Him you shall serve."

(Matthew 4:10 NKJV)

"Confess that 'Jesus is Lord.'"

(Philippians 2:11)

"Why do you call me, 'Lord, Lord,' and don't do the things I say?"

(Luke 6:46 NIV)

This last verse is important. Jesus is asking why we call him Lord, but do not allow him to be in control of our actions, attitudes, and thoughts. What does a *lord* do? He's the boss, the CEO, the master. He's in charge; he calls the shots and makes the decisions. He has authority and control over us. We want to remain in control of our lives because we always have been—until we met Jesus. We're used to doing things ourselves.

My husband is a Type A temperament, make that a triple A, and a very natural leader. He *enjoys* being in charge. I like that because I can relax, but there are two times when even he feels out of control, and it is not a good feeling: when he gets lost in an unfamiliar place (and his work involves extensive travel) and when he's taking care of a baby. Babies sometimes get out of control—and none of us, even doting grandpas, know how to fix them. The other kind of person who wants control is a fixer. I fall into that questionable category. A fixer is someone who wants to avoid conflict by heading it off before it happens, fix things when problems arise, avoid hurt for other people, and keep peace at all costs. These are good goals but are sometimes inappropriate. A fixer tries to be everybody's mediator or savior. We can misguidedly "love" so much that we get in the way of our loved ones knowing the Lord more fully.

Taking control is sometimes motivated by fear or by self-focus. It is not always comfortable or easy to take our hands off. We foolishly think that if we relinquish control, things will fall apart—as if it's up to us. Wrong. That's self-focused thinking. Even when we relinquish our eternal destiny to God and receive his salvation, we still struggle with control in certain circumstances. For example, when:

- We forget that God's timing is perfect and he doesn't seem to work fast enough.
- We don't understand or like the way God is working.
- We feel like God has taken a long vacation from us, and if anything is going to happen, we will have to handle it ourselves.
- We misconceive God as a sort of toy maker, think Geppetto to Pinocchio, who winds up his creations, gets them going, and then is uninvolved.
- We put God into a spiritual "compartment" in our lives, a Sunday-only friend.

The truth is, God *is* our life, intimately involved in every detail we experience. When and how things occur is preplanned by him. He deserves our absolute submission to his loving control.

Five: Let Go of Your Comfort Level

My precious little curly-headed granddaughter, Shae, has a "blankie" she calls her "soft." Her mother and I made several small blankies for her when she was a baby. No deal. Shae latched on to a fringed decorator throw with a toile print on one side and satin on the other and at least three times Shae's size. But that doesn't matter.

When it is not in its designated place when needed, the universe stands still for Shae. It is what brings her comfort.

All of us, even as sophisticated adult women, carry around "blankies." They're in the form of our own comfort levels in life. How might that appear? A life that requires very little effort, no stretching, little vulnerability, no change of habits and activities, and certainly no venturing into uncharted territory. But, to get up and get going in the morning-of-life means that we must get out from under our secure, comfort-level quilt. Our being a growing and going believer in Jesus Christ means that we must *intentionally* get up and get a bit uncomfortable, and be available to God.

When I was a child, our one heater was on the wall between my bedroom and my parent's bedroom. In between and throughout the rest of the house was an unheated hallway with a cold cement floor. It was hard to get out of my warm bed and go down the arctic hall. But I soon learned that when I made myself get up and moving, I didn't stay uncomfortable for long. I stretched, I moved, I got going, I got warmer; I got busy living life. There is a funny verse in Proverbs 26, describing a lazy person with a foolish excuse to remain in bed, inactive, unproductive, with his silly claim that there might be a lion, a risk, in the street. This lazy guy claims that it would be much better to stay where he is, safe and comfortable.

As believers, God asks us to give up, to let go of our own comfort level, and allow him to stretch us as we serve him. Do you feel God's "push" on your heart to do or to be something for him that's not comfortable or easy, that you're not sure you can even do? I do.

A familiar quotation contains a very practical truth: "If we keep on doing the same things we've always done, we'll always be the same way we've always been." We can easily drift through our entire lifetime settling for less than God's best for us. Let's pray for each other that we'll get up and get serious about being and doing everything God wants us to do, and that he'll enable us to stop pushing and pushing and pushing the spiritual "snooze" button that keeps us dozing off back into our comfort zone.

Six: Let Go of "Things"

Imagine you are out in your yard talking to a neighbor while your toddler sleeps peacefully upstairs, then you notice smoke coming from an open window. What would you rush in to save? Your new couch? Your favorite bedspread or flower arrangement? Would you try to pull up your new carpet or remove your new kitchen cabinets? Does too much of our thought life focus on *things*? How drastically would our joy, our peace, our quality of life, our sense of self-worth be affected if we didn't have all the things we have? How much are we affected right now because of the things we *don't* have—and want? Philippians 3:7–8 teaches us that the value of a person is not determined by the things he possesses and Colossians 3:2 tells us to, "Let Heaven fill your thoughts. Do not think only about things down here on earth." We need to let go of things we have, or things we would *like* to have, that mean too much to us. That's *hard* to do.

We've been warned about living lives that enable us to "gain the whole world" (and all its stuff) while losing our own soul. We've heard about the foolish person who tears down his barn because it is too small to house everything he has accumulated, and then finishes building a bigger barn to store it all on the day he dies. When Donald Trump goes into eternity, his multitude of possessions will have no more bearing upon his eternal destiny than upon the homeless man living on the street below one of his high-rise hotels.

When my son Mark was ten years old, he visited missionary friends in Kenya. There were few toys, no television, no computers, no video games, no transportation, and "nowhere to go"; he played with sticks, rocks, grass ropes, and vines. He had space to run, magnificent butterflies to chase and black mamba snakes to watch out for (Mom worried about that idea). It was a highlight of his life, in spite of the absence of all we think we need for a certain quality of life.

If we are truly trying to prioritize our life and loves, God will show us what we can personally do to rid ourselves of excess "stuff" and replace it with service and love—and contentment and gratitude for all that we have in Christ Jesus. He will enable us to live lives of *open-handedness*—always ready to give to everyone he places in our path, every time he prompts us to.

One time my daughter Jenifer and I spent an enjoyable mom-and-daughter day at our local mall. On the way home, we swung by our favorite sandwich shop. After waiting for our order, topping it off with a couple of chocolate chip-macadamia nut cookies, we pulled out into traffic and got caught by a red light at the intersection. Jen began to unwrap her sandwich when she noticed a frail, older lady on her right, holding a cardboard sign reading, "Hungry. Will work for food". Jen rolled down her window and handed her sandwich to the lady, who smiled weakly and headed for the curb to have her unexpected lunch. Jen, a teenager at the time, simply said, "I really wasn't very hungry, Mom."

A few months ago, Jenifer was at the busy music store where she worked. Helping an attractive, well-dressed lady, Jen commented on the woman's pretty red purse. After paying for her purchase, the woman asked for an extra plastic bag and dumped the entire contents of her expensive purse into it. She handed the purse to Jen and said, "I want you to have this. I have lots of other purses." The generous woman left the store, carrying her new plastic bag purse as if it were a Gucci. Truly, what goes around comes around. *Things* seem pretty trivial, don't they?

There's one more thing God asks us to let go of. We're going to save it for last. Right now let's consider what God asks women to *hold on to*.

What Does God Ask Us to Hold On To?

An image from the terrible South Asia tsunami of December 26, 2004, sticks in my mind. Unknown numbers of people, from a three-year-old boy to the supermodel Petra, spent days in the water holding on to debris, literally for dear life, until they were rescued. We need to hold on to priceless gifts of eternal value which are infinitely more important than life itself. As we do so, it is God himself whose hand is really holding us. Isaiah 41:10 tells us, "Do not be afraid, for I am with you. Do not be dismayed, for I am your God. I will strengthen you. I will help you. I will uphold you with my victorious right hand."

Several years ago, my family and I lived in Dodge City, Kansas, the town of Wyatt Earp, Miss Kitty and the Lone Star Saloon. One morning we awoke to a fresh covering of newly fallen snow. As Jim and Mark ventured out to the car to make our way to church, Jim said to Mark, "Hold on to my finger, son, so you won't slip and fall." Dutifully, Mark caught hold of his daddy's strong finger and the two began the risky trek down the front steps together. It was a sweet, tender moment—until Mark lost his grip and tumbled down the steps.

Jim later said that he had learned a dynamic lesson that day. The big strong daddy is the one who should hold on to the little child, not the other way around. The child is simply not able to cling tightly enough to be safe and secure. In like manner, God holds on to us as his little children, and we can count on that.

> "My sheep know my voice; I know them and they follow me. I give them eternal life and they will never perish. No one will snatch them away from me, for my Father has given them to me, and he is more powerful than anyone else. No one can take them from me. My Father and I are one."
>
> (John 10:27–28 NASB)

As God holds us, who and what should we hold on to? We must focus on the Person of God, the Plan of God, the Power of God, the Presence of God, the Peace of God, and the Provisions of God.

One: Hold On to the Person of God, Jesus Christ

The book of Hebrews gives us a wonderful promise and an important instruction:

First it promises, "That is why we have a great High Priest who has gone to heaven, Jesus the Son of God. Let us cling to him and never stop trusting him" (Hebrews 4:14); then it tells us, "And since we have a great High Priest who rules over God's people, let us go right into the presence of God . . . Without wavering, let us hold tightly to the hope we say we have, for God can be trusted to keep his promise" (Hebrews 10:21–23).

Why Should We Hold On to Jesus?

Because he is life. If Jesus were removed from your life, what would you have left? "In Him was life—and that life was the Light of men" (John 1:4 NIV); "I am the Way, the Truth and the Life" (John 14:6 NIV).

In a recent television interview, a Hollywood correspondent representing the community of the stars was bragging about the emergence of interest in religion and spirituality among their ranks. She thought it was "wonderful" that the superstars were connecting with their "inner selves" through yoga, transcendentalism, and a variety of alternative spiritual channels. However, she had difficulty explaining why Christian principles are so often met with criticism and outright antagonism among the ranks of the stars, while most everything else goes.

The false messiahs, alternative "prophets," or leaders of other religions not founded upon Jesus Christ have all died. They will always be physically dead, but the Bible says of Jesus, "Therefore he is able to save completely those who come to God through him, because he always lives to intercede for them" (Hebrews 7:25 NIV). We hold on to Jesus because he is life. All religions, all expressions of spirituality, do not lead to the same place, but "He that has the Son has life" (1 John 5:12 NIV).

Because he is love. The first Bible verse many of us ever learned and taught our own children is, "God is love." The lyrics of the first song we teach our children about God are, "Jesus loves me, this I know, for the Bible tells me so." Over and over in Scripture, we are told about God's unfailing, never-ending, unconditional goodness, and love. Psalm 92:15 promises: "He is my rock and there is nothing but goodness in him." Psalm 59:10 says, "In his unfailing love, my God will stand with me. He will let me look down in triumph on all my enemies." God gave us the capacity to love each other when he created us in his image, and what a gift that is!

In the midst of hurricane Katrina (September 2005), which ravaged New Orleans and the Mississippi Gulf Coast, there were incredible stories of people who gave up seats in helicopters and rescue boats to allow needier people to receive the treatment they desperately needed. One large Asian group of citizens relinquished the right to be rescued and chose to be the "last people out" because they had love and compassion for other needy people. Love enables people to even give their own lives for others, in Christ-like gestures of selflessness.

There is an often-told story about two little brothers who were close in age. One of them desperately needed a blood transfusion and when a donor match was searched for, his younger brother was a perfect fit. Arrangements were made for a transfusion, and the two little boys were placed side-by-side on a hospital bed to make the life-giving transfer possible. As the one little brother's healthy blood flowed into the body of the other, the donor lay still with his eyes tightly closed. Finally, the transfusion completed, the brother who gave his blood to his desperately ill brother asked the attending physician, "Doctor, when do I die?" He had sincerely thought that the giving of his blood to his brother would cost his own life, and he was willing. The greatest of all loves is the love that Jesus has shown toward us. "Greater love hath no man than this . . . that a man lay down his life for his friends." That's us. The "friends of God," by his priceless grace. If God had a picture on his desk, it would be of you; a name etched across his heart, it would be yours. He's never too busy to spend time with you; nothing you say or ask seems trivial to him. When you use his gifts to create or design—to organize or achieve—he's as proud as punch. He's the greatest fan in your cheering section, and you can hear him unashamedly shouting out your name in total support, whether you win or lose. The Lord of Love absolutely *adores* you. Hold on to Jesus.

Two: Hold On to the Plan of God

Sometimes God's plan for us is clearly stated in Scripture and understood in our minds. He tells us to go, he tells us to love, he tells us to forgive. But sometimes God's plan is a little cloudy, as we "see through a glass darkly." It's sort of like when I've worn a pair of contact lenses beyond the suggested two weeks and I need to throw them away and get a new pair. We prefer the clearly defined and delineated version of God's plan most of the time, but God often chooses the I-want-you-to-trust-me plan. Remember the beautiful, prophetic story of Abraham and his precious son, Isaac, the promised son he had waited so long for?

Abraham's real-life story took place centuries ago, but many of us can relate to elements within it. There was a physical move to an unfamiliar place, family struggles, promises of God that seemed too long in coming. There were "silent" times when God's divine hand could not be seen or his plan understood. Sometimes, matters were taken into human hands, resulting in unnecessary problems, complications, and pain for all involved. There was the arrival of a beloved "late in life" child. There was much praying and waiting on God by choice or necessity—and the incredible experience of the Lord's presence and provision.

At God's instruction, Abraham had loaded up his wife, servants, belongings, herds, and family pets to move to a new land, Canaan. Abraham apparently, and understandably, had some apprehension about such a seemingly "blind" move, and when the Lord appeared to Abraham and promised "rewards" for his obedience, such blessings seemed incredulous. The acquisition of earthly rewards hit a tender spot in Abraham's heart, and he expressed his concern openly and honestly to God in Genesis 15:2 and 4, "O, Sovereign Lord, what good are all your blessings when I don't even have a son?" The Lord went on to explain to Abraham that he would provide "a son of your own to inherit everything I am giving to you." This was amazing since Abraham and his wife were old, they were laughably beyond the optimal, or feasible, childbearing years.

As promised, the treasured child, Isaac, arrived on the domestic scene where the blessed old couple had long awaited this answer to their prayers. Their joy was surely indescribable. They must have marveled at every tiny smile, every new accomplishment, each amazing stage of development in the life of their adored son.

Then, right in the middle of the years of joy because of the Lord's gracious provision, God instructed Abraham to offer that precious son as a burnt offering—a sacrifice—on the altar of Mt. Moriah. Once again, God's words seemed absolutely incredible. What Abraham's limited human perspective could not envision was that the loving Lord of all creation, the maker of young Isaac, had already provided the "real" sacrifice—a ram caught in a thicket near the altar. Even as God asked of Abraham something so hard to even imagine, he had already provided the very resource that would make obedience possible. Beyond that, through the compliance of the son and the agony of the father, the Lord painted a beautiful prophetic masterpiece of his own sacrificial substitute for the sins of Abraham, Sarah, Isaac, you—and me.

God's plan for Abraham, Sarah and Isaac was much better than Abraham had anticipated. In a similar manner, Ruth and her mother-in-law, Naomi, went through a time in which God's plan made no sense, and the two women had no idea how their very difficult situation would turn out. When we first meet this unlikely duo, it is not in the light of a negative depiction we so often see between a mother-in-law and her son's wife, these two ladies are homeless, destitute widows, bound together by their mutual tragedies. Circumstances look so bleak and so hopeless, but in the midst of them, Ruth chooses to bind her life inseparably to her late husband's dear mother and to commit herself wholeheartedly to Naomi's great God.

As a result of her righteous decision we see an amazing adventure unfold and a moving love story emerge throughout the pages of the book of *Ruth*. The God of all resources provides for Ruth and Naomi's physical needs, all the while creating the family backdrop and ancestral lineage through which would come the Messiah we love and serve today.

God makes a promise to us in Jeremiah 29:11: "For I know the plans I have for you, declares the Lord, plans for good and not for disaster, to give you a future and a hope." That's all we need to know, more details are not necessary.

What Do We Know for Sure about the Plan of God?

God's plan is good. We know that God's plan for us at every time, in every situation, is good, always and forever.

God's plan is to make us more like Jesus. His primary purpose is not to make us comfortable or successful in the sight of other people—but according to Romans 8:29, "to become like his Son."

God's plan is eternal. "And I am sure that he who began the good work within you will continue his work until it is finally finished on that day when Christ Jesus comes back again" (Philippians 1:6). God started his plan when we came to him for salvation and he will continue to work in and through us until we are with him, complete, in everlasting Heaven.

God's plan for us is personal. In my own life, two songs have impacted me by reminding me of the good plan God has crafted for me. The words of Isaac Watts's famous hymn speak for me when they say:

When I survey the wondrous cross
On which the Prince of glory died,
My richest gain I count but loss,
And pour contempt on all my pride.

Were the whole realm of nature mine,
That were a present far too small.
Love so amazing, so divine
Demands my soul, my life, my all.

The other song, *His Way, Mine*, touches my heart and reminds me that I am committed to doing the will, and following the great plan, of God for my life.

God has a will for every planned creation—a path for every star to go.

He drew the course for every river's journey, now I know he has a way for me.

I place my life in the hands of God—those hands once scarred, now outstretched for me.

Wherever it may be, over land, over sea—May thy will divine, Oh, thou God divine, be mine.[6]

When I learned that song as a college student, I envisioned God's plan for me as an ever-upward rising tower—reaching greater heights, going and growing straight up and up, achieving wonderful things for God's glory and his great kingdom. Upward, always, ever upward. But God's wonderful plan for my life—and the lives of all I love so much—has often looked more like the journey of a roller coaster. *Up, up, up*—mountaintop view. Wait. We're going down. When do we start having fun? Whoa, slow down a little. I want off this ride, right now. Yes, we're headed up again, and more slowly. Good. Oh, no!—Now I remember what happens when we get to the top again. In spite of the high points and low points and everything in between, God's great personal plan has been good just as he promised. I wouldn't have wanted to miss the smooth, easy roads, or the rocky, curvy, treacherous ones—he's been my absolutely dependable driver the whole time, and he will bring us safely to our wonderful final destination.

Jesus is our Master Sculptor, he shapes us, molds us, lovingly, carefully, painstakingly, chipping off the many rough edges and polishing us up like the diamond-in-the-rough we are; the diamond that looks a lot like coal at times. He works on us while hearing our constant objections, "Oh, that hurts—no, not that way," or "Just leave that part of my life alone and don't try to fix it, please."

God's primary plan for my life and yours is to make us more like Jesus, and, unfortunately, in my case, the two pictures don't match yet. The rest of God's plan for my life may look more like that upward graph or it may look more like the roller coaster, but it will be good, either way.

Three: Hold On to the Power of God

We tend to underestimate who God is. We often see God as an indulgent "grandfather" who is at our every beck and call and who offends us when he doesn't give us everything we have on our wish list.

We might picture God as a faraway, absentee creator who started it all and wound up the key, but then let the universe just take its course, including our lives. He is quite uninvolved and unconcerned.

Or we imagine God to be a white-bearded judge in a long black robe with a very large, threatening club in hand, watching and waiting with glee to see us fail and fall. He's eager for us to mess up so that he can have the opportunity to "straighten us out."

We can believe deeply in God, but fail to see him as the wonderful God of awesome love and matchless grace that he truly is. We serve a powerful God who has revolutionized millions of lives, and he has broken the slavery of addiction, restored crushed lives and broken homes, replaced hate with love, and hopelessness with expectation.

My husband has a tattoo on his left arm that he is not proud of. It says, *Mi Vida Torsida,* My Twisted Life. He got it before he received the awesome power and grace of God that *untwisted* his life, and turned him into a servant of Jesus Christ; now he is a preacher of the gospel, a wonderful husband and father—and a "Papa."

Listen to the psalmist: "But as for me, I will sing about your power. I will shout with joy each morning because of your unfailing love" (Psalm 59:16). Listen to the apostle Paul: "But this precious treasure—this light and power that now shine within us—is held in perishable containers—that is, in our weak bodies. So everyone can see that our glorious power is from God and not our own" (2 Corinthians 4:7). We need to hold on to this mighty power of God.

Four: Hold On to the Presence of God

How do we hold on? The most important way is to focus on Jesus through prayer. As believers we constantly function in the realm of his presence, but we need to be *aware* of his presence with us at all times. Paul continues to tell us in 1 Thessalonians to pray without ceasing. Nonstop praying! You may think, "Are you kidding? I can't be constantly on my knees—nothing would ever get done around here." Let's look at what Paul means. Sometimes the prayers we voice or think to God are specific, because we have a special need or desire that we want to bring to him—that we sincerely want him to do something about. I could honestly say, "everything I learned about prayer I learned from kindergarteners—my own three, and those in the classroom—they just pray and believe." Most of the time, *voilà*; the answer comes in the affirmative. Our daughter, Lisa, prayed for a baby sister or brother, a big prayer of faith when that looked like a slim-to-none possibility. We have Jenifer as a direct result of her prayers.

Sometimes our prayers aren't verbal prayers, sometimes they are nonverbal times of communication and fellowship when we just enjoy the closeness of our Savior Jesus who lives in us. It is as though Jesus moves into the home of our heart and from then on, the door between us is left open, like leaving the door to our children's room open so we can hear what's going on and so they can hear us.

In any relationship there are communication lapses—times when it is hard, for one reason or another, to talk to each other. When we *do* say something during those times, we can't think of much that's positive to say so we just don't talk much for a while; sometimes a long while. We start to feel unloved or unworthy, and our minds start imagining the worst, fearing what the silence might mean. But, when communication is good, we talk spontaneously whenever thoughts come to our mind, easily and often—but there are also times of silence then too. However, when the relationship with that other person in our life is warm and loving, the silent times are times of love and unspoken fellowship too. The quiet times don't seem at all like a threat anymore. Silence can communicate too.

That's what it means to pray without ceasing. To always be in a spirit of communication with our very best Friend, our Savior, our Redeemer, and our God. It is not a matter of completing a task and thinking, "Okay, I prayed, I said my amen, I'm through for the day."

When our son Mark was a kindergartener, he took swimming lessons at the local YMCA. One day I was delayed in picking him up. By the time I arrived at the usual pick-up point, he was nowhere to be seen. I began to feel concerned, not so much for Mark's safety but because I knew he would be disturbed and confused. I searched throughout the building until I opened the door to the women's locker room; there knelt Mark by one of the benches. When he saw me a look of relief came over his face and he said, "Mommy, I was just asking God to help you find me."

What was Mark feeling that morning after swimming? Lost, alone, betrayed, foolish, vulnerable, afraid, worried, confused, inadequate, discouraged, sad. Have you ever felt any of those? If you're like me, you encounter those emotions at one moment or another every day. It is at those moments when we can hold on to the presence of God and pray to our Lord:

> Please help me, Lord. Show me what to do next.
> I can't handle this, Lord, you're going to have to.
> I'm sorry, I made a big mistake. I really did wrong, Lord, and now I've created a mess. Please compensate for my sin and lack of judgment.
> I'm feeling really discouraged today, Father. It's a beautiful day but that's not helping any, Lord. Be with me.
> I'm so worried. Help me know that this situation will be okay—ASAP.

We have lots to pray about all the time, don't we?

One time my grandson Micah prayed and finished it by saying, "the end." We should never really say "the end" to our personal prayers. To live in the presence of God, our life should be an open-ended conversation with our Savior from the day we meet him in salvation until we talk with him face-to-face in Heaven.

Five: Hold On to the Peace of God

My husband has a reproduction of a painting; you've probably seen one like it. It is a picture of a lighthouse in the middle of a terrible storm. Huge waves are crashing on the shore. The tiny silhouette of a man stands in the doorway of the lighthouse, watching the storm, right in the middle of it—and obviously safe in spite of it. You could probably testify of that peace in the middle of a storm. Perhaps it was job loss or serious illness or errant children. How did you do it? The Bible instructs us to "be still and know that I am God" (Psalm 46:10). When we tell our children to be still, we usually mean *sit down* and be still. With children, standing seems to be synonymous with moving, jumping, bouncing, twirling, and spinning; so when God tells us to *be still* and know that he is God, we might think, "How in the world can I ever do that? Nothing will ever get done around here while I'm trying to be still." But God doesn't say, "Sit down and know that I am God." We can "be still" when there is much going on around us, just like a baby asleep in his parent's arms. When Mark was a baby in California, we experienced a strong earthquake; I jumped in terror and ran to his room, and there he lay, sound asleep. However, we know from personal experience that to be at peace like a baby is not easy for us adults. We've lived longer and are more aware of *what if*s. But, as hard as it is to be still and know that he is God, we can focus and refocus on God's sufficiency to meet our every need, and our peace will increase and abound. Focus on Jesus. Trust him in peace.

Six: Hold On to the Provisions of God

There is one last vitally important thing that God asks us to do; he wants us to hold on to the provisions of God. What does this mean? The provisions of God are closely linked to the promises of God. All that he promises he will provide, and what he tells us he will perform; he promises that his provisions will be there when we need them. Do you really believe that? It's true.

There is a principle in Scripture that, though it is not named this, could be called the principle of prior provision. That simply means that God will supply all of our needs from his wealth of glorious riches, which have *already* been given to us in Christ Jesus (see Philippians 4:19). At the right time, he can and will provide a job, a car, strength, patience, hope, endurance, comfort, grace, groceries, and a mortgage payment. When a need arises it does not catch God by surprise and send him scrambling to do something about this unexpected, upsetting problem we are experiencing. He never says, "Oh, dear! I've got to figure out some way to fix this—and quick!"

God knows our need is coming and already has provisions in place to meet that need from his always-stocked storehouse of supplies. Meeting our need is not difficult for God, he will deliver exactly what we need, at the right time and in just the right way.

At times, I've felt a little twinge of envy for my single-mom friends. If you're like them, then often—by choice or not—you are absolutely dependent upon the Lord for your every provision. Many of you have been through tough experiences in which you have seen God work personally and powerfully—you have *learned* that he will provide. I've learned much from the lives of believers who know the power of God to provide, and they trust him to meet every need. Then he does provide for them, often visibly and dramatically, as a mighty visual display to others, like me, who observe.

Isaiah 65:24 is a powerful verse which gives us a promise we can "hang our hat on": "I will answer them before they even call to me. While they are still talking to me about their needs, I will go ahead and answer their prayers."

Holding On to Salvation, Letting Go of Guilt

Perhaps we think that our greatest need for "provisions" is in the physical realm. But is that true? I believe that what you and I need most is God's incredible provision for the forgiveness of all our sins. We need his redemption, the everlasting life he promises, which God has *already* provided for us through Jesus Christ. We are told in 1 Timothy 6:12 to "Take hold"—to hold on to—the gift, the provision, of eternal life.

As we consider God's provision for all our needs, we need to pick up where we left off, and consider those things we must let go of. What is the last and most important thing that we need to let go of? God tells us to let go of *guilt*; we need to let go of guilt over past sins, regardless of what they were. The apostle Paul was a murderer,

David was an adulterer and an instigator of murder, Abraham was a liar, and Jacob was a conniving cheat, but the Bible says, "There is, therefore, now no condemnation to those who are in Christ Jesus" (Romans 8:1 NKJV).

I grew up in a time when we used chalkboards instead of white boards. It was the honored job of the board monitor to erase the day's work from the blackboard. Then the erasers were taken outside and banged against the sidewalk around the school to clean them. The monitor got to wet a big sponge and wipe every last bit of chalk off the board, until the board looked brand new. That's exactly what Jesus did for us when we prayed and asked for his gracious forgiveness of our sins. He wiped the blackboard of our hearts completely clean from all sin; he missed no spots. In scripture after scripture he assures us that our sins are totally erased, they are gone, invisible.

When Satan accuses and torments us over a past sin that shames us constantly, the one we so desperately regret and wish we could change, God looks lovingly at us and says, "What sin?" Divinely, it is as if we had never, ever sinned—not even once. By his mercy and grace, he chooses to completely forget our sins, for all eternity, and to make our hearts brand new. Therefore, we need to let go of guilt. Jesus paid the price for our sins and made us brand new people. Old things are passed away; all things have become new. We need to let go of guilt over sins, mistakes, missed chances, bad choices, and hold on to the provision of God for forgiveness and salvation through Jesus Christ our Lord.

Phillip Yancey depicts an inspiring scene in his book, *What's So Amazing About Grace*, as he describes the lives of several worshipers who participate in a communion service together. As I read his moving account of real people whose lives have been changed by the power of God, I pictured believers whose lives have crossed mine over the years and whose testimonies of grace inspire me daily:

> Imagine with me that you are leaving the church after an inspiring Lord's Supper service—a wonderful time of communion you have

experienced between you and your Lord. As you exit the building, you notice other believers who have silently worshiped with you in the presence of the Lord himself.

There's Pam, a hat covering her bare head, scarred from the surgery in which the doctors had removed a disfiguring brain tumor. Pam's eyes are filled with tears as she remembers the loss of her young son the year before in a boating accident and thinks of how God himself suffered the loss of his only son. Pam, Jesus' precious blood was shed for you.

Robin, a leader in your church's drug rehab program, follows Pam out. Jesus completely revolutionized Robin's life. He was transformed from a hopeless addict into a bold minister to those whose plight he understands so well. Robin, Jesus' precious blood was shed for you.

Your eyes fall on Rita, married three times, once to a man who tried to end her life. Rita, whose life was plagued with guilt over past mistakes until she met Jesus Christ. Rita, Jesus' precious blood was shed for you.

Then came Penny, a young mother of two whose heart aches as she recalls the abortion she had many years ago—and the Savior who forgave all her sins and made her brand new. Penny, Jesus' precious blood was shed for you.

Near the end of the line of exiting believers comes young Sarah, recuperating from the recent pain of giving birth—out of wedlock. Sarah placed her beautiful baby boy into the eager arms of his welcoming adoptive mother. Sarah, Jesus' precious blood was shed for you. What is your name, dear lady? Friend of Jesus, his precious blood was shed for you.[7]

> There is life in the blood of the Lamb Who was slain.
> There is power, there is power in His name.
> There is love pouring out of the wounds that were made,
> Pouring out, pouring over our shame.
> So praise the God Who saves.
> Praise the God Who bled.
> Praise the God Who was nailed to a tree—
> And wore our sins upon His head.[8]

Chapter 5 Study Questions

1. All of us, even as believers, have difficulty relinquishing control of our lives in practical ways. Depending upon our temperament, personal "history," situations we face, and where we may be in our spiritual journey, most of us tend to "hold on" to fear, anger, hurt, expectations, a desire to control, a personal comfort level, or things we have or want. Ask God to help you see if you are having difficulty letting go of any of these areas of your life, or if there is anything else that you are holding on to that keeps you from full surrender to Jesus Christ and "resting and trusting" in him. Then, "let go" of it, as often as you need to, until you are completely his.

2. Some things to which we hold so tightly are not of real value, and other priorities that we hold very loosely and carelessly count the very most now and for all eternity. What sustains, inspires, and strengthens you most in your Christian walk, besides the person of God himself: God's plan, God's power, God's peace, God's people, or God's provision? Take time to thank him for all he's done for you and all he means to you.

3. Why do you think it is so hard for us to open our hands and hearts and let God be our "Everything?" Ask him to show you ways that you can release your hold on everything that's of little or no worth, and to learn to hold tightly, and consistently to his promises and presence in your life.

4. If you would like to do a personal study using this chapter's topic, here are some Scriptures you may want to refer to:

Hold on to	Let go of
Psalm 21:13; 59:16; 119:117; 139:10	James 1:21
Proverbs 4:18	Acts 18:9
John 10:14	Ephesians 4:31
Romans 5:1	Hebrews 8:12; 10:17; 12:1, 15
Philippians 4:19	Luke 11:12
Hebrews 3:6; 4:14; 10:23	1 Peter 5:7
Ephesians 2:14	Philippians 3:7–8
1 John 5:11, 20–21	Colossians 3:2
1 Peter 3:11	1 John 4:18
1 Thessalonians 5: 21	2 Timothy 1:7
Acts 1:8	Psalm 56:3
Ephesians 3:20	Psalm 103:12; 115:11; 118:6
	Proverbs 3:5, 6
	Isaiah 41:10, 13; 43:1, 5, 25; 44:22; 53:5; 64:9
	Jeremiah 31:34

Lead/Follow

Lisa

Think of some well-known "odd couples" in popular culture. Mutt and Jeff, Tom and Jerry, Laurel and Hardy, Felix and Oscar, Miss Piggy and Kermit. They are odd teams that work well together (and are entertaining). I personally like to see an odd couple come together; I think it's fascinating. I look at the couple and wonder what brought them together and how in the world they have learned to co-exist in each other's completely different world. I try to analyze what they have to offer each other and what makes the relationship work.

Women are faced with an "odd couple" virtually every day. This couple has a known success rate when joined correctly. They have a lot to offer each other, and they work in perfect harmony when both parties are in tune. The odd couple I'm talking about is actually one of the hardest things God asks a woman to do: to follow and lead.

Follow and lead. Lead and follow. An odd team, but one member doesn't seem to work without the other. In case you are wondering which team you are on, you are on both. You are both a leader and a follower, regardless of your personality type. Keep reading; I'll show you what I mean.

God Asks Women to Both Lead and Follow

No matter how you look at it, leading and following cannot exist without co-existing. You cannot be a host or hostess without guests. You cannot be an owner of something without a product. You cannot be a follower unless you are following something or someone. Conversely, you cannot lead anything or anyone if no one is following you. Leadership expert John Maxwell says, "He who thinks he leads, but has no followers, is only taking a walk."

Leadership and "followship" go hand in hand. While they have some distinct differences, they are more alike than what you may think. Beauty and the Beast were both looking for love, Felix and Oscar were both fanatical about their points of view, and Piggy and Kermit were both self-absorbed. Leaders and followers share some real similarities.

For example, just because you are a leader, that doesn't guarantee that you will be a good one. Think of some of the very worst leaders: Hitler, Saddam Hussein or Osama Bin Laden. These men would fall under the category of leaders, but were they good ones? Certainly not. It's not necessarily hard to be a leader, but it's much more challenging to be a good leader. And followers are not always good followers. Thankfully, many followers of leaders like Bin Laden and Hussein have defected, but obviously not all of them.

Let's bring it closer to home. What about us as Christian women? We are literally "followers of Christ," but are we? Do we represent the type of person who would follow Christ, stand for what he does, and emulate him? We'll look at that shortly, but let's think about the subject of being a leader first.

God Asks Women to Lead

When God asks a woman to lead, what does he expect? Perhaps when you think about leadership you identify it with the Type A people of the world, people who are driven, or outspoken, or aggressive. Those who are quiet, introverted, or passive are disqualified in our minds when it comes to their ability to lead, but this is not always the case.

Leadership in Action

God gave us two great examples of women in the Bible who were very different in temperament from each other, yet both showed leadership in action. If you blinked, you might have missed one of these women because she is only mentioned in a few passages in the Bible. Her story is much more obscure than that of the other woman we are going to look at; the other woman's story has an entire Old Testament book devoted to her. Both stories are amazing and inspiring: one woman was an official, the other was royalty. One led with a gavel, one led with a scepter, but both women deserve to be in the Women of Leadership Hall of Fame.

Deborah the Judge

The story of Deborah is told in Judges 4 and 5. Deborah was the fourth and *only* female judge of Israel raised up by God. She was, from birth, a dynamo. She came into this world with a blast, and she grew to be a unique and strong-minded woman who was a wise and skillful leader with a remarkable relationship with God. She was a wife. She was a prophetess. She was an agitator. She was a fearless ruler. She was a warrior, and in a great twist of irony, she was also a writer and a composer of poetry and songs. Deborah used her natural gifts and talents as a leader to impact others with her discernment and confidence in God. Deborah is one of the outstanding women of history.

Queen Esther

And then there was Esther. Esther was a more reluctant participant in this leadership thing. Nevertheless, her story is so important and so meaningful that an entire book of the Bible is named after her. We're told that Esther had great outer and inner beauty. She was a patriot. She risked her life for her people. She was a queen, but even with her favored position, she was not to approach the king to speak with him without his permission. She wasn't guaranteed that her request to meet with him would be granted, so she was a strategic risk-taker, not in a reckless way, but in a confident way. Because of Esther's courage and faith, she single-handedly saved her nation from genocide. She was a true leader.

Deborah and Esther were leaders; they both led physically. Yet, they led differently: Deborah was loud, large, and in charge—born to lead and loving every minute of it, while Esther was quieter, and being a leader of her people was something she not only did not seek out, but also it was out of her natural comfort zone.

I have always loved playing the piano. My mother put me in lessons when I was very young, and I continued with them until well into my teenage years. For me, playing the piano was a hobby. I would go to the piano and sing my heart out while playing sappy love songs. Although I had been trained in theory and the technical aspects of being a pianist, I was not very interested in scales or beats per minute or rests or anything that involved details. Once I learned to play, I just loved to play for fun, and my piano teacher knew it.

One time in high school, my piano teacher asked me to do something that was really a stretch for me, "Lisa, I need you to do me a favor. I have inadvertently committed myself to play at two different places on the same day, and I need you to go to one of those in my place. I can't make it to both."

I nervously waited for her to tell me exactly what she meant by that and hoped I could pick which of the two events I would do, but she picked for me. "I need you to go to the First Methodist Church and accompany their choir for the offertory song on Sunday. Will you do it?" Suddenly, I couldn't answer. I quickly began to do what most of us do when we want to get out of something that doesn't sound very appealing; I tried to think of an excuse, any excuse, but my mind was totally blank. I could not think of a single excuse that I had ever used for a late homework assignment or to get out of a date or anything. So after a moment passed, I heard myself saying, "Well, sure, Marie, I'd be happy to." I hung up the phone, went into the bathroom, splashed cold water on my face and took some Benedryl for the hives I was already getting.

Sunday came sooner than I wanted it to. I drove over to the First Methodist Church. It was one of those large all-stone churches with the graveyard attached to it, and seeing the graveyard made me more nervous than ever. I was so intimidated by all of it. This choir was counting on me to accompany them, not hinder them and here I was, the girl who didn't like beats per minute, taking the place of an accomplished pianist with years of experience. I was in way over my head. I had no choice but to do it; I was already committed. Despite my nerves it was going to happen, so with very sweaty palms I walked to the stage and played. I did what I had determined to do, and it worked out. Was I uncomfortable? Oh my! Did I miss some notes? Oh yes! But it wasn't a complete disaster, and I made it through.

The important thing was not that I played for a choir that day, but that God had stretched me to do something I didn't think I could do. He used me despite my insecurities.

We get comfortable in places and situations that are familiar to us. We don't like to do things that require a lot of stretching or stepping out. That's why we generally gravitate toward the same people and the same schedule and the same scenarios everyday. We're creatures of habit, and we get comfortable in our "assigned" roles. We get used to being the quiet one or the loud one or the outspoken one or the peacekeeper or whatever the case may be. Even in your family of origin, as you grew up, you probably had a role that you played in the family. And we still play roles. For those who aren't natural leaders, you assume that means that you don't ever need to lead—you're off the leadership hook, and you pass that buck on to someone else who either wants or clearly needs to lead, because being a leader is not an easy thing, and you know it. It takes courage.

When you lead in some way, you put yourself out there and make yourself vulnerable; you open yourself to scrutiny. In 1 Samuel 10:26–27 it talks about how, when Saul was anointed king, the men who had once been his closest companions suddenly became his most outspoken critics. Since leaders are out in front of others, they often have people judging them or becoming jealous of them.

The question then becomes this: Should we limit ourselves to what comes easily? Should we be leaders if we are better at following? Well, certainly, we should be who God created us to be, and we can't all lead all the time. Make no mistake about it, leaders need followers, since too many cooks in the kitchen is chaos. But that's not what we are talking about here. It's really about being prepared for God to use us in any capacity, even if it is not natural for us or is out of our "comfort zone."

God used Deborah, an assertive and decisive woman, to lead, but he also used Esther, a reluctant leader with a more passive personality. And he used both in a mighty way.

Not All Leaders Are Good Leaders

When we actively lead, it can be a positive position with positive results, or it can be used in a negative way with negative results.

An old folktale is told about a small village in the Bavarian Alps where they had a significant problem; the town was completely infested with rats. The townspeople had tried virtually everything to get rid of these rats, but nothing worked. So the town officials spread the word that there would be a reward for anyone who could get rid of the rats and take care of this problem once and for all. A man came forward and promised he could rid them of this problem; they in turn promised the prize if he did.

The man, called the Pied Piper, started playing his instrument. Low and behold, the rats started coming out of the cracks and crevices. They began to follow him, out of town to the edge of a high cliff. The Pied Piper stood at the edge and played while the hypnotized rats fell off the cliff, one by one. Problem solved.

This mysterious musician went back to the town officials and said, "Okay, I've done it. I've gotten rid of the rats for you. I want my reward." But the town officials decided not to honor their word; they would not pay the reward. The Pied Piper determined he would get even with them, and started playing a new tune on his flute. This time, all the children of the town came out of their homes, and the Pied Piper walked into the woods with the children following him, and they were never seen again.

Not all leaders are good leaders.

It says in God's Word that one day all of us will face the Bema seat, the judgment seat of Christ. I don't know about you, but that worries me a little bit because I know that I have not lived in a perfect, Christ-like way. I am certainly not a "perfect" Christian. No one is. But I think I would rather be me than to be David Koresh or Jim Jones on judgment day, wouldn't you? They were two of the most heinous cult leaders in recent history. They both led large numbers of people to self-destruction.

You and I may never have the opportunity to lead in action, like Deborah or Esther, but we are all leaders in at least one way. In some capacity, we all lead in attitude.

Leadership in Attitude

As Christian woman we are leaders in our homes. We can make our homes a place of peace and emotional strength, or we can make our homes a place of strife and contention. But not all women who lead are married. Those who are single and may never be a wife or a mother are still leaders emotionally to those around them—in the workplace, in the community, in our schools, and with friends and family. We can have a monumental impact on the lives of others.

Leading in Our Homes

Ever heard the phrase, "If momma ain't happy, ain't nobody happy"? If you are married, and have been for any length of time, your husband has probably thrown this statement out a time or two. We laugh when we hear it, but for those of us who are wives and mothers, we realize we are the emotional compasses of our home. If we aren't doing well, neither is anyone else.

No matter what our personality is like, we control the emotional climate of our homes. We are emotional leaders in the home, and with leadership comes responsibility.

If you are a CEO, you can't say to the company you work for, "I'll take the salary and the insurance and the benefits package, but I cannot be responsible for the future of the company. I'll have to defer to someone else on that." It doesn't work that way. Just as a CEO holds the responsibility for the company he oversees, so we are responsible for the emotional tones we set in the areas we oversee, in the family, and in the home.

Can you think of any worse place to live than on a roof or in a hot, dusty desert? Yet the book of Proverbs tells men that it would be better to live on a roof or in a desert than with a woman who leads the home in an emotionally negative way. "It is better to live on a corner of the roof than share a house with a quarrelsome wife" (Proverbs 26:24). "Better to live in a desert than with a quarrelsome and ill-tempered wife" (Proverbs 21:19). Think of it: a home with climate-controlled air, fluffy pillows, and soft blankets is a *less* desirable place than a roof with hot shingles, or a desert with gritty sand, and one hundred degree temperatures. It's that big of a deal; emotional leadership in the home has that much of an impact.

Leadership in the World

Phoebe, Dorcas, and Lydia were all women mentioned in the Bible who led with attitudes that glorified God. Many women have started movements across the world that had emotional impacts on others: Florence Nightingale, Susan B. Anthony, and Corrie Ten Boom.

Clara Barton was a single woman with a lot of influence. Though never married, one person once said that Clara Barton was "wedded to her convictions." Out of her desire to serve and help soldiers on the battlefield, she nursed them as they lay dying, at times even in her arms. Her kind and generous ways were the catalyst for the movement known today as the American Red Cross.

Aimee Semple McPherson is credited with starting the Four Square Movement in America out of her overwhelming desire to see lives changed by the power of the gospel of Jesus Christ. Her physical leadership grew out of a heartfelt emotion and a steadfast determination to influence others to experience God's love. She led first with her attitude.

The name Mother Teresa is synonymous with that of "servant-hood." As a young nun, she was so impacted by the suffering she saw outside of the convent walls that she devoted her life to serving the poor. Probably no other woman in history has had such an enormous impact on our view of service to others than she has. Many have followed her example and given their lives to reach out and help the less fortunate of this world.

Don't underestimate the power you have over what happens emotionally in the lives of others. But the truth is that, oftentimes, we cannot be the leaders we are supposed to be because of our own frailties. A lot of us are broken, scattered, and needy. We are weak emotional leaders because we are weak emotionally; we must get our lives filled up by God so that we can be the emotional leaders to others that God meant for us to be.

How do good leaders act? In today's society, we often choose leaders based on their looks, their wealth, their popularity and appeal, and their willingness to do anything and everything to get to the top, but are these really the traits we should desire in a leader? And if we ever get the opportunity to lead, what will be required of us?

The Six R's of Leadership

There is an abundance of books and materials on leadership, and there are many "experts" on leadership, but I am not one of them. After doing some research and using my own personal experiences, I have come up with a few thoughts of my own about what it takes to be a good leader. My Six R's of Leadership for the Christian woman are by no means an exhaustive list of characteristics, just a few that I feel are the most important.

1. Recognize (who you are). When you lead, you must know yourself: your strengths, your weaknesses, and the experiences that have made you qualified to lead.

You are exactly who God created and put together. David reminds us of this when he says:

> For you created my inmost being;
>   you knit me together in my mother's womb.
> I praise you because I am fearfully and wonderfully made;
>   your works are wonderful,
>   I know that full well.
> My frame was not hidden from you
>   when I was made in the secret place.

When I was woven together in the depths of the earth,
     your eyes saw my unformed body.
All the days ordained for me
     were written in your book
     before one of them came to be.

(Psalm 139:13–16 NIV)

Who did he create you to be? What are your areas of strength? What are your areas of weakness? Pinpoint and identify who you are and where you function most effectively, and what role you flourish in.

We all make up the body of Christ, and we are all important to that body. Part of recognizing who you are is determining what gifts God has given you, and that makes a good leader. If you don't know who you are or where you're coming from, how can you expect others to? If you don't know what your spiritual gift or gifts are, you need to find out. Read 1 Corinthians 12 and seek spiritual guidance from older Christians.

2. Respect (others). Everyone needs and wants to be validated and encouraged.

Everyone desires to be heard. In 1 Peter 2:17 it says, "Show proper respect to everyone: Love the brotherhood of believers, fear God, honor the king." We honor God and are more effective leaders when we show respect to everyone, whether they deserve it or not. When you lead, you must listen to people, and consider their thoughts and ideas. Most of the time people will respect you if you respect them. Good leaders are not just goal-oriented but also people-oriented.

3. Recall (the mission). When you lead you must ask yourself this question: What am I trying to accomplish through my leadership position?

Good leaders always keep in mind why they are leading and what they are leading for. They know who they are and what they are all about. Don't let anything distract you from your message or your cause. Every successful company has what they call a mission statement; it states the core philosophy of who they are and what they are all about as an organization. Have a personal mission statement. Have a clear understanding about what you are leading for. We are exhorted in 1 Corinthians 15:58 (NIV) to "Let nothing move you. Always give yourselves fully to the work of the Lord, because you know that your labor in the Lord is not in vain."

4. Reject (pride). When you lead, you must recognize that it's not about you. Don't let it be.

There's no room for self-focus or self-indulgence in leadership. Pride will get you in tons of trouble when you are trying to lead. It will hinder you and cause you not to see clearly what needs to be accomplished. Proverbs 11:2 has this to say on the subject: "When pride comes, then comes disgrace, but with humility comes wisdom." It doesn't mean you can't be strong, but you must be humble.

5. Recruit (people). When you lead you must resist the tendency to do everything yourself.

When you are capable and self-sufficient it is hard to delegate to other people to get the job done, but it is important to do just that. Deuteronomy 1 talks about how Moses, the strong leader of the people of Israel, appointed helpers from each tribe to assist him. He said in verses 9 and 13, "You are too great a burden for me to carry all by myself. Choose some men from each tribe who have wisdom, understanding, and a good reputation, and I will appoint them as your leaders." Rather than trying to handle all the larger responsibilities by himself, Moses made a wise decision to share the load with others. This also allowed them to have the opportunity to exercise their God-given gifts and abilities.

6. Rely (on God). When you lead you must ask God for guidance and wisdom.

Depend on him, and draw upon his strength. Psalm 121:2–3 reminds us, "My help comes from the Lord, the Maker of heaven and earth. He will not let your foot slip—he who watches over you will not slumber;" God will guide you as you lead, if you rely on him. A good leader realizes pretty quickly that he or she does not adequately have the courage and the wisdom to lead others if their resource is not that of Jesus Christ. He alone makes it possible to be an effective and good leader.

Staying Focused

One day you may be asked to serve as the head of a finance committee or lead a Bible study or head up an accountability group. Lead with zeal in your home and in your circle of influence, but as you do, remember the six R's and practice them so you can lead in the way God wants you to. When you look at the leaders around you, in your church, at work, or anywhere else, make sure they also have these qualities, and always, always test ideas coming from leaders against the truth of God's Word. What they are proposing should never draw attention to themselves.

When Leonardo da Vinci had painted his *Last Supper*, he asked a friend for an evaluation. The friend heaped superlatives on the masterpiece and especially praised the wine cup by the Lord's hand. At that point, Leonardo da Vinci blotted out the cup. "Nothing," he was said to have answered, "should distract one's attention from the Lord." [9]

All the Reimers have terrible vision. My dad has trouble with his eyes, and so does my mother, my brother, my sister, and myself; we all wear contact lenses or glasses. I have worn contacts for nearly twenty years. It seems as if we were all basically born "blind as bats." We often joked, as I was growing up, that if there were a fire in the house in the middle of the night, or if for some reason we needed to evacuate our home, we would be the blind leading the blind trying to get out of the house. None of us can see without some serious help.

As capable as any of us are, and as determined as we might be, our leadership on this earth is really like the blind leading the blind. In our human bodies and with our limited minds and abilities, we are totally incompetent in comparison to our heavenly leader, God.

We are fallible people, but we follow a completely capable and competent Father.

The bottom line to leadership is this: when you lead, whether it is in action or in attitude, let nothing distract you from God. Some leaders can speak persuasively and yet not direct you towards God, they direct you towards themselves. In Deuteronomy 13 it tells you to beware of false prophets who try to lead you astray. A leader should never want or need to take the glory for a success or an accomplishment, because outside of Christ, we can accomplish nothing. We have to stay focused on him.

God Asks Women to Follow

So, what does it mean to follow?

My mother and I taught a seven-week class on *The 7 Hardest Things God Asks a Woman to Do* to a group of women at our church. The first week we surveyed the women and asked them to tell us what they thought were some of the hardest things God had asked them to do in their life. Most of them had the same basic theme. Some of them talked about "letting go and letting God," some mentioned difficulties with surrendering to the will of God, and a few even used the "S" word (submission). They were all referring to the same exact "hardest thing." It is the same thing that Christ asked of Peter and Andrew as he came across them casting their nets into the water to fish. In Matthew 4:19 he said to them, "Follow me, and I will make you fishers of men." He asked them very simply to follow him, and he is asking Christian women to do the same thing today. You can call it letting go. You can call it surrendering. You can even call it that dreaded word submission, but it all boils down to following God. Following God is our mission, our passion, our yearning, and our struggle in life, all at the same time.

When I was a senior in college, I became very fascinated with a person I saw on a fairly regular basis. His name, I came to find out, was Joe. From what I observed, Joe didn't have many friends, except for one friend he always had with him. They walked to class together, went to chapel together, and even crossed the street together. Joe let his friend be his leader, because it was his only way of knowing where to go. Joe was blind, and his friend was a guide dog.

Jesus wants to be our eyes for us as we struggle blindly through life. One of the hardest things he asks us to do as Christian women is to let him be our guide. Following Jesus seems as if it should be the easiest thing in the world for us to do. Why would we not want to follow such a capable, all-knowing, ever-present, loving God of the universe? How could we not trust him? We say that we do, but despite our intentions there is this one thing that gets in the way every time. It's a four-letter word, W-I-L-L, our will. Our will gets in the way of his will for our life.

I've heard it said that following God is the ultimate expression of how much we trust his providential hand. It's about trust, it's about dependence, and it's about faith. As the poet Mary Brainard once wrote, "I would rather walk with God in the dark than go alone in the light."[10] It's in our moments of darkness that we see how much trust and faith we really have in God, but most of us women have a hard time giving up control.

Though it may be hard, we must realize that the Lord is calling us, as Christian women, to surrender our will to him. We have to let go and let God if we are going to truly be followers of Christ. He's asking us to raise the white flag and finally say, "Okay, Lord. I surrender my all to you; you're in charge." Yet we're more likely to think of submitting as saying, "Okay, fine, lock me up; I give up; I submit."

Ironically, some people in prison have finally gotten quiet enough to meet Christ, and as a result they finally have gotten free. Paul could rejoice in the midst of his physical imprisonment. He was okay, because he had ultimate freedom through Christ. Many of us are physically free and not locked up in a cell somewhere, but we are locked up on the inside because we are still trusting in our freedom and haven't let God be who he needs to be in our lives. What we fear the most, giving up control, is what we need the most. Submission to God brings freedom, not confinement.

The apostle Peter talks about the submission of the believer when he writes:

> Submit yourselves for the Lord's sake to every authority instituted among men: whether to the king, as the supreme authority, or to governors, who are sent by him to punish those who do wrong and to commend those who do right. For it is God's will that by doing good you should silence the ignorant talk of foolish men. Live as free men, but do not use your freedom as a cover-up for evil; live as servants of God. Show proper respect to everyone: Love the brotherhood of believers, fear God, honor the king. Slaves, submit yourselves to your masters with all respect, not only to those who are good and considerate, but also to those who are harsh.
>
> (1 Peter 2:13–18 NIV)

Submitting to God—following God—requires that we not only agree to submit to him, but also to submit to other authorities he has placed over us. Does that make us second-class citizens? Not at all. We belong in the "chain of command" right where he wants us to be when we are following him.

Three Key Ways We Follow Christ by Following Others

The Badge and the Believer: Following God requires that we follow the rules of government.

Have you ever tried to get a parking spot at Wal-Mart on a Saturday afternoon? All the shoppers in the world have made their way to the same Wal-Mart you are going to and at the same time. As you circle the parking lot looking for a space, frustrated because you just need to run a quick errand, an idea pops into your head. You aren't legally handicapped in any way, but the only parking space you see open is one for the handicapped. And you begin to rationalize, "I just need to get two items. It will only be ten minutes tops. What's the real harm in it?" So you circle around one more time, and then park.

It's the minor rules we compromise. God tells us we must submit to the rules of government and follow them, regardless of how we feel about them. The only time we would show exception to this is if it is in direct violation of a law of God; he is the highest and ultimate authority on every subject. Submitting to the authority of government is really submitting to God.

Pews, Pulpits, and People: Following God requires that we follow the leadership of the church.

I heard about a man who couldn't understand why his young son didn't want to attend church anymore. He and his wife would drag the boy to the church every Sunday and then bribe him to go in. One Sunday they got fed up and asked him, "Son, why don't you want to go to church with us?" The boy replied, "Why would I want to go somewhere where the building is too cold, the service is too long, the preacher is too loud, and the people are too nosy?" The parents looked at each other and said, in unison, "Where did you hear that?" And he replied, "From the backseat of our car."

Do you realize the impact you have as a follower of the church's leadership? Whether in a small church or a large church, your "followship" can either help or hinder the way ministry is carried out in the body of Christ. Are you the one who encourages and uplifts the ministers or leaders by supporting them with your words and actions, or are you all too often guilty of being the complainer, the critiquer, or the cynic? When we join a congregation of believers, we need to be committed to following and submitting to its leadership.

Does this mean we have to agree with everything that goes on? No. Do we have to endorse everything we see and hear? No. Even church leaders can be wrong and misguided, but because Christ holds these positions up to the highest standards and responsibilities, if the church leaders are wrong, God will deal with them. It's not our job. Our responsibility is to follow their leadership, unless and until it contradicts the leadership of God.

Who's the Boss? For married women, following God requires that you follow the leadership of your husband.

I recently taught a class about marriage at our church, and I titled the part on submission, "The Elephant in the Closet"; it's something we'd rather keep hidden and not discuss. Do you want to kill a ladies' party? The next time you go to a cooking party or jewelry party or candle party, bring up the subject of submitting to your husband. You will either clear the room or incite a riot. Women are passionate about this subject. Because this book is not about marriage we are not going to spend a lot of time on this issue, but if you are a married woman, it is vitally important to follow Christ and his mandated leader, your husband. Following the leadership of your husband is following and submitting to the authority of God. Though not referred to before in this chapter, make no mistake that this issue is included in the passage in 1 Peter about the submission of the believer, and in other key passages in Scripture. In 1 Peter chapter 3 verse 1, the apostle says definitively, "Wives, in the same way be submissive to your husbands."

A few years ago our family went to Disney World. We were excited to get there, but in the middle of the first day we began to sense rain. The clouds rolled in, and all of a sudden it became a downpour. I mean cats, dogs, horses, and cattle fell from the sky. There we were, stuck in the middle of the magic with no umbrella. Suddenly, off in the distance, I saw a bunch of big colorful umbrellas in the middle of some tables; we made a mad dash for one, got under it, and let it cover us. While the rain fell all around us, we were staying dry under the shelter of the umbrella. In the same way that the umbrella provided relief from the rain, submission to our husbands is for wives a welcome shelter and protection.

For many of us wives, our view of being submissive to our husbands tends to be somewhat skewed. We look at is as intrusive, controlling, humiliating; but it is not. Submission requires strength, not weakness. It takes courage. It requires a strong belief and trust that God knew what he was doing when he established this "chain of command" back in the days of Adam and Eve.

So, we follow God and submit to him by following the leadership of government, following the leadership of the church, and following the leadership of our husbands.

The Six R's of Followship

But what qualities does it take for us as Christian women to not only be good leaders, but also good followers? We discussed the six R's of leadership, so now let's look at the six R's of followship. Here they are: recognize, respect, recall, reject, recruit, rely. Wait. Didn't we already cover these? Do these sound familiar? Yes. I mentioned at the beginning of this chapter that I was going to show you how the two "paradoxes" of leading and following relate to each other in a unique way. Ironically, leading and following come together like Mutt and Jeff because they share the same qualities. Different roles, but with the same character traits.

1. Recognize (who you are). When you follow, as in leadership, you should know both your strengths and your weaknesses.

Keep in perspective who you are, not in comparison to others, but in comparison to who Jesus is. This will encourage you to be the kind of follower you need to be.

2. Respect (others). When you follow, you must respect others.

How can you possibly follow the leadership of government, the church, or your husband, without respecting them, their role, and their authority? Christ has, after all, put them in that position, and we must have reverence and respect for our leader, Jesus Christ. Respecting those you follow is the core of submitting to them and to him.

3. Recall (the mission). When you follow, you must recall your mission. Your mission in life is to follow Christ. Don't ever lose sight of this.

4. Reject (pride). When you follow, you must not let pride block you and hinder you from being a truly effective follower.

When pride gets in the way, following someone seems cumbersome, tedious, and confining. It doesn't allow the freedom and joy of being a follower to come in. You simply must reject pride in order to be a successful follower.

5. Recruit (people). When you follow, you must recruit others.

Our life as followers of Jesus Christ must have a strong emphasis on recruiting others to come to a saving knowledge of the Father. We are to give witness and testify to what he has done in our life, and what he wants to do in the lives of others. We should never horde the blessing that comes with following Christ, but rather, share it boldly with others. When you believe in something strongly enough to follow after it, you cannot keep it to yourself.

6. Rely (on God). When you follow, you must resist the natural tendency toward self-sufficiency. If we don't rely on God, we won't follow him; plain and simple.

Isn't it interesting that Leadership and "Followship," Mutt and Jeff, with their seeming contradictions, have the same basic characteristics? If you are a believer, you are a leader and a follower at the same time; these positions both require a total dependence upon Jesus Christ; an unwavering faith and trust in him.

I love the book of Hebrews; it is so rich in its truths. I especially love the "faith chapter"; it inspires and moves me every time I read it. It talks about many people—men and women—their unwavering faith in God, and the result it had. Leadership and "Followship" are really all about one basic thing: faith, not faith in our abilities, not faith in government, not faith in our husbands, not even faith in the church. Leadership and "Followship" are really all about faith in God. That's it, that's all.

I ran across this definition of faith in my husband's study Bible, and I thought it was really good. It says: "Faith is confidence that someone or something is reliable." We must ask ourselves: Do I have confidence in God? Do I believe that he is reliable? I thought about what would happen if the faith chapter in Hebrews had included me in it. What would it say about me? I thought about some of the things I might want it to say:

"By faith, Lisa, because she loved God, trusted him with the ability to handle her life. She did not fear for the bills to come, but left them in the capable hands of God."

Or,

"By faith, Lisa, because she had confidence in God, gave to him an offering of her time. She relied on him to provide for her the strength and discipline to get it all done."

Or,

"By faith, Lisa, although she was tested, trusted God with her three small children. She let go of the burden of making sure they all turned out perfect."

What would you want the faith chapter to say about you? What does it say about who you are as a leader, and a follower?

Faith, submission, surrender, leadership, followship—it's really all about how much you trust God.

Chapter 6 Study Questions

1. Spend some time this week searching your heart to see if you are disqualifying yourself from leadership. Are you ignoring something God wants you to do out of fear of rejection or scrutiny? Ask the Lord to help you determine if and when he wants you to lead. Ask him to help you be open and willing to get out of your comfort zone or "assigned" role.

2. Examine any obstacles that might be in the way of you being a good emotional leader in your home. Identify them and give them over to God, asking him to provide you with the strength and trust in him you need to overcome them. Ask him to bless your home with harmony and peace, and to fill you up emotionally as only he can.

3. Determine what you believe following is really all about. Examine how you feel about issues like faith, trust, dependence, surrender, and submission.

4. Write your own definitions of these words and look up at least one Scripture passage for each. Submit yourself to the scrutiny of the Holy Spirit and ask him to show you areas of your life where you need to give yourself to him and his will for your life. Ask him to give you the peace and faith to rest in him.

5. Read the faith chapter in Hebrews, chapter 11. What would it say about you if it were written today. What would you want it to say? Are they the same, or different? Give the Lord your full attention and commit anew to him that you will pray and strive for greater faith in your life.

6. If you would like to do a personal study using this chapter's topic, here are some Scriptures you may want to refer to:

Leadership

Exodus 3:1; 6:9–12; 17:10–13; 39:42–43

Deuteronomy 1:9–18

Joshua 1:1–5

1 Samuel 10:26–27

1 Chronicles 21:8

1 Kings 2:5–7; 12:15–19

2 Kings 15:18

Nehemiah 1:1; 3:1

Isaiah 3:14

Matthew 15:13–14

Acts 6:3

1 Thessalonians 5:12–13

Hebrew 13:18–19

Followship

Exodus 13:6–9

Numbers 16:13–14

Deuteronomy 27:9–10

Matthew 4:18–20

Luke 9:62

Mark 3:7–8

John 1:38

1 Corinthians 10:2

2 Thessalonians 3:9

1 Peter 2.21

Revelations 13:3; 14:4

Die/Live

Kathie

My husband, an avid hunter, gave our young son Mark a BB gun. One day I watched from inside the house as Mark and a neighborhood friend did some target shooting. A sparrow perched in a nearby tree caught their eye. As if the hunting gene was in his blood, Mark took aim and the tiny bird fell to the ground, mortally wounded, amazing both the boys and this mom. For a moment, there was much whooping and backslapping. Just as quickly the mood became somber. The two tenderhearted boys stood looking at the motionless bird. Then Mark sprinted into the house and asked for some string and a small box. "Mom . . . I shot a bird," he said weakly, mustering a weak smile to convince both of us that that was a good thing. I glanced at his face and saw his eyes filled with tears. I hugged him and gave him his supplies. I watched with overflowing emotions as the two boys dug a hole, put the sparrow in the box, and buried it in the backyard. They tied sticks into a cross and conducted a funeral service for the deceased victim. They had seen the face of death for the first time in their young lives.

Before becoming aware of the inevitability and finality of death, a child knows that to "die" means to lie still and not get up, and that it's serious. But they also see lots of cartoons in which Sylvester the cat, Wiley Coyote, or whoever Bugs Bunny is tricking at the time, gets flattened by a bulldozer or falls off a zillion-story skyscraper. In the next scene, however, the unfortunate victim is fine and furry again, ready to retaliate.

My own children never really liked scary movies, and that was okay with me because I didn't like them either. But when my daughter Jenifer was about ten or twelve she spent the night at a friend's house, and against her better judgment she watched an old black-and-white zombie movie. She later recounted how even though the movie had no special effects that characterize action flicks today, it was the scariest thing she had ever seen (we're a pretty wimpy family). People who had died were still walking around! What a scary thought. Actually, that is going on right now. Today, millions of people who have "died" are more alive than ever, and it's not at all scary; in fact, it's wonderful. I am one. I hope you are too.

God Asks Women to Die

There are two categories of people who inhabit the world: those who are physically alive but spiritually dead, who have never come to Jesus for life; and those who have "died" to themselves and are now very much alive in Jesus Christ. Have you died in Christ and come alive?

I pray that every one of us has already died to our old life, our old self, and our spiritual obituary has already been written (see Romans 6:6–11). According to Romans 6:4, many of us have even been buried, and incredibly, now we are not zombies but brand new people, walking and living. Amazing!

Voluntary Surrender

Our spiritual obituary shows the cause of our death as "voluntary surrender," and that's the hardest thing God asks us to do; to choose to die to ourselves. Indeed, that sums up everything else that is "hard" that he asks us to do. Because God has us exercise our will, at some point in time we have to give up our sins, our ownership of self, and seek our own way to God. When we relinquished these so-called rights, the sin and guilt we had been carrying around   the "person" we were by our very basic nature—died. Died, dead. *Good and dead.* Good riddance.

A horrible early punishment for murder definitely would have been a deterrent to all who witnessed it. A victim's body was strapped to the back of the one who had murdered him. As the body decomposed, the decay spread to the killer and eventually he died too. That makes the apostle Paul's words all the more profound. Listen to Romans 7:24: "Who can deliver me from this body of death?" Paul says that the only One who could deliver him, and us, from the awful weight of that body of sin we carry throughout life is Jesus.

At the instant we surrender our lives, our sins, and our will to Jesus Christ, an amazing divine "exchange" takes place. Our old, guilty, spiritually dead self dies, and his new divine life becomes alive in us. "Therefore if any man be in Christ, he is a new creature: old things are passed away; behold, all things are become new" (2 Corinthians 5:17 KJV).

Refusing to Surrender

But some people won't surrender that "body of death" they are carrying around.

Nearly thirty years after World War II ended, on March 10, 1974, Lieutenant Hiroo Onoda finally surrendered his rusty sword, as the last Japanese holdout to give up arms. In 1944, when Lt. Onoda was sent to the island of Lubang in the Philippines, he was told to defend it at all costs—and defend it he did. For twenty-nine years people tried to persuade the lone soldier that the war was over and he should surrender, but he would not. Finally, after Hiroo Onoda received a personal letter from his commanding officer, he was willing to give up the fight.

How sad and unnecessary. Mr. Onoda wasted most of his adult life in I-won't-surrender-no-matter-what mode. Even more sadly, many people live just like that in the spiritual realm. We don't always overtly and dramatically express our resistance, or our rebellion, but often subtly, quietly, willfully we guard the kingdoms of our lives that we consider our own. It was not easy for Mr. Onoda to relinquish control since he had lived a life of "no surrender" for a long time. To change meant a radically altered lifestyle, though the difference between the two types of existence were only a few miles apart.

Many of us who have been privileged to grow up in church are familiar with a hymn with this challenging message: "All to Jesus, I surrender. All to him I freely give." That's it. I give up, I surrender all to him. That's what salvation, forgiveness, and eternal life is all about.

A television commercial shows a family seated together in a room to hear the reading of a deceased elderly relative's will. The attorney inserts a video and the rapt audience sits stunned as the woman related, in a video she had made before her death, stipulations about how her inheritance should be divided among the heirs. One by one each family member is addressed, with the requirements that must be met before anyone would inherit a dime of her estate: a grandson must cut his hair and dress better, a nephew must get a decent job, and on and on.

When we come to Jesus Christ for forgiveness and eternal, abundant life, it must be with no stipulations; no strings attached by us. We sign a blank contract. That is why we are to come to him like little children. Children have no expectations, no complicating doubts and fears, no holdbacks and worries about "what if." They don't think, "Whoa. I'd better read all the fine print in this eternal contract and see if it fits with my plans." A child simply trusts this Lord who is absolutely trustworthy. A child comes simply, willingly, with his whole heart and soul, when Jesus tenderly calls.

My grandson, Graham, recently prayed at bedtime with his mother and gave his life to Jesus Christ. When the simple prayer for salvation was concluded, Graham summed up immediately what that surrender meant to him. Graham spontaneously began to sing, loudly, and convincingly, "Yes, Lord, yes, Lord, yes, yes, Lord. Amen." That's it. So simple. So eternally significant.

When we come to Jesus through the death of our own will and our own plans for our life, we come through: 1) His willing surrender and death on the cross, and 2) our willing surrender and death to self. Then we find *life*. Those believers we all love so much who have physically died are very, very much alive right now. But they live in a new and much better location. Jesus is their life.

Satan Wants You to Die Too

Ironically, Satan also wants us to die; spiritually and eternally. Definitely not in the sense of dying to ourselves as Jesus asks of us. What does the devil want to destroy? He wants to destroy our soul. How can he do that? Here are some of Satan's tools.

- He misrepresents who we really are and what our spiritual condition is really like.
- He tries to kill any of our desire to make changes.
- He gets us to compartmentalize "faith"—to keep it separate.
- He destroys relationships.
- He minimizes our effectiveness.
- He entangles us in addictions and habits.
- He makes us think that we know everything.

- He preoccupies us with other things.
- He gets us to procrastinate until it's too late.

Marlon Brando was a mega-star in his day. Dark, handsome, the bad boy of adventure and intrigue; he did and had everything that stardom provides. But at the end of his life, addicted, scarred, broken, bitter, unfulfilled in spite of all his acquisitions and accolades, Brando made an appalling statement in his last lucid moments of life. When asked how he would sum up life as he looked back over all his achievements, Marlon Brando said, "What was that all about?" Life had no meaning, no purpose, no satisfaction, no fulfillment—just a life-full of chance, random happenings and a great deal of hopelessness and pain. Life to him, and to many like him, was only death. He missed it. How sad.

In contrast, the apostle Paul, who exchanged his dead life for victorious life on the road to Damascus, explained what happened to him. "I have been crucified with Christ and I no longer live, but Christ lives in me. The life I live in the body, I live by faith in the Son of God, who loved me and gave himself for me" (Galatians 2:20 NIV). Jesus said, "If you lose your life, you save it. If you die to yourself, you live." If, given a choice to live for yourself or die to yourself, your tendency is to choose to live for yourself, *Beep!* "Wrong answer!" the apostle Paul tells us.

The Spiritually Dead Person

So, what does a spiritually dead person look like? We might think, "Oh, that's easy. He's the guy wearing a black trench coat with his hair spiked into devil's horns." Or "the tattooed girl wearing very little, but what she does have on is all black, and even her make-up looks evil." But what about the kind of person described by Paul in his letter to the Galatians, "When you follow the desires of your sinful nature, your lives will produce these evil results: sexual immorality, impure thoughts, eagerness for lustful pleasure, idolatry, participation in demonic activities, hostility, quarreling, jealousy, outbursts of anger, selfish ambition, divisions, the feeling that everyone is wrong except those in your own little group, envy, drunkenness, wild parties, and other kinds of sin. Let me tell you again, as I have before, that anyone living that sort of life will not inherit the Kingdom of God" (Galatians 5:19–21).

A few of these descriptions sound a little too familiar to us, however, so we move quickly on through the list because we remember that this list is the "bad guys" and we're the "good gals." Still, the question mark remains in our mind: "You mean quarreling, jealousy, angry outbursts, selfish ambitions, envy, thinking that my little circle of friends are the only ones who are right—those practices are really bad? Aren't those just part of normal human life?" Yes, "normal" for people without Jesus alive in them. Uh, oh.

It's easy for us to imagine spiritually dead people as those who choose Satan's way instead of Jesus', and those who reject Jesus Christ in some overt display of rebellion and resistance to him. Sometimes that does happen, with a person willfully turning away from Jesus. But what about the nice soccer mom next door? None of us chooses to be spiritually dead. Most people haven't even been offered the gift of life to the point where they might say, "Nah . . . I don't want that." We don't have to *do* something to belong to Satan. We are automatically his.

"For all have sinned and fall short of the glory of God."

(Romans 3:23 NKJV)

"But God demonstrates His own love toward us, in that while we were still sinners, Christ died for us."

(Romans 5:8 NKJV)

"For as in Adam ALL die, even so in Christ all shall be made alive."

(1 Corinthians 15:22 NKJV)

"He who believes in Him is not condemned; but he who does not believe is condemned already."

(John 3:18 NKJV)

Remember, there are only two categories of people—dead and alive— both physically and spiritually. We don't choose death; we've already got it. We must *choose life,* or it will never be ours. The reason that point needs to be emphasized is that it's a constant struggle to see people around us as they really are. We're not alive because we've been so good that we deserve to live. None of us is righteous, not one. We receive life by God's grace alone.

When we first moved to Charlotte, North Carolina, we lived next to great neighbors. We had children and grandchildren about the same age; our houses and yards were about the same size, and we came and went on similar schedules. I thought that Jan and Bob went to church, but I wasn't sure. Day after day I wondered about their spiritual condition and day after day passed without my finding out. Finally we decided to move from the neighborhood to another part of town, and I began to pack up our belongings. Again I wondered about Jan's spiritual condition, and feeling very guilty, I trekked next door to finally find out.

I got there at just God's appointed time; Jan was home, but not busy. We engaged in small talk and eventually, about spiritual things. Jan was interested, very interested. As I shared God's wonderful plan of salvation with her and asked if she would like to receive God's free gift of eternal life, Jan said quietly, "Yes. Yes, I would." Together we prayed, hugged, and shed a few tears. Then Jan, church-going Jan, said to me, "I never heard that before. Thank you."

God Asks Us to Give Away Life

If we have life, how can we pass it on to people like Jan? How does giving away "life" tie in to the other hard things we've looked at in this study of what God asks us to do?

- We must have our single focus on Jesus. Opportunities often come at unexpected, busy moments, and if our focus is on anything else we may let them slip by with precious eternal lives in the balance.

- To walk with Jesus and be his witness, we must juggle the spiritual multi-tasks of being grateful, content, mindful, gracious, real, and a servant. We need to live without the grumbling and complaining that would turn others from the positive, blessed gospel of Jesus Christ. We must love without hypocrisy. We must be willing to lose personal esteem in the eyes of one who deserves the opportunity to say "yes" or "no" to Jesus Christ. We must be a servant; we earn the right to be heard when we serve.

- We must be both tolerant and intolerant. People without Christ act like people without Christ.

- We must be a successful failure. Our "success" is based upon our willingness to "fail" as we present Jesus Christ to other people.

- We sometimes need a strong dose of the Lord's patience and insight as we wait on his perfect timing to share our faith with those he places in our path. More often, he must give us a gentle, or firm, spiritual "push" to get us to boldly proceed as he opens doors of opportunity.

- We must confidently hold on to the assurance that he will give us boldness and the correct words, as we share our faith with others. At the same time, we must let go of pride, expectations, and the desire to gain "personal points."

- We must follow and lead. We must follow God's lead, to lead others to him.

Sharing our faith can be one of the hardest things God asks us to do, and Satan wants to keep that from happening at all costs, but it can become our spontaneous daily lifestyle with Jesus, the Life, living and speaking through us.

How Jesus Raised the Dead

The New Testament tells us how Jesus spread life among the people with whom he came in daily contact. In those accounts we see three ages of people he raised from the dead, which can serve as models of three stages of how people react to his offer of new life.

Jesus gave life to children. In the wonderful story of Jairus's young daughter (Mark 5:21–43), Jesus restored to life a child whose life had just begun, and then ended. Entering the home of the little girl, Jesus passed by the devastated family and friends of the child. The crowd of mourners did not easily accept Jesus' words of comfort that she was "not dead . . . only asleep." Inside the room where the girl was lying, Jesus touched her hand and simply, lovingly, told the child to "get up." Simple as that. She opened her eyes and "woke up."

It was easy for this young child to come to life. She had not been dead long and the marks of death were not very evident. She was still at home; no burial arrangements had been made. When Jesus gently spoke life to this little girl, she instantly awoke from her sleep of death, and as is so characteristic of growing children, she was hungry. Jesus, aware of the needs of every "child"—regardless of age—instructed them that the little girl, now so full of life, be given food. For children, responding to the voice of Jesus is logical, reasonable, and appealing. They get it. What could we possibly hold on to that would equal life? Why would anyone, ever, choose death over life? Yet, that happens every day in a million scenarios. So many times those who make such an illogical choice by overt decision or careless neglect simply have not been presented with the consequences or eternal benefits of their rejection or acceptance of Jesus' incredible offer. That's where we come in.

Not only do we sophisticated, over-educated, know-everything adults need to spiritually become like little children, we also have a tremendous opportunity to impact reachable, teachable children in our families, neighborhoods, churches, and communities. What great opportunities we have to share Jesus with the children, and the other child-like hearts he loves.

Jesus raised teens to life. In Luke 7:11–17, the tragically sad story of a teenage boy's death was compounded by the fact that he was the bright star in the life of his single mom. He was her only child, her only hope, her only help in her coming old age.

The marks of death were more evident in this story than with Jairus's daughter. The teenager's body had already been prepared for burial and the funeral procession, with its professional grievers voicing the mother's great loss, was snaking its way through the onlookers. Hopelessness was almost tangible as Jesus pressed through the crowd and brought the procession to a halt.

Then Jesus did the impossible. He brought the boy to life. Amid all the noise, the tumult, the obstruction of the crowd—the voices, the pulls, the distractions—life *still* came to the teenager. Amazingly, teens will still freely come to Christ when they are privileged to know of his great love and grace given to them. Their spiritual, life-changing decision may occur in the very midst of peer-obstructions of all kinds—and the marks of their spiritual death may be more evident to those who know them—but teens will come gratefully to Jesus Christ when given the opportunity.

Many of us have much more influence upon young men-and-women-soon-to-be than we realize. They observe much more than they admit, they listen more than their demeanor shows, and they are open to the life provided by the infectious, unconditional love of Jesus Christ. What an awesome opportunity for those of us who know him. What a critically important time in the lives of young people who stand poised on the brink of bright potential for life and eternity.

Not only was the widow's son a vivid picture of a teenager in great need, but he also was a graphic example of who we all are without

Jesus. We are spiritually dead, absolutely helpless in our own efforts to become "undead." We can do nothing; not be good enough, not think enough positive thoughts, not do sufficient good deeds. Our spiritual condition is irreversible without Jesus.

Jesus raised adult people to life. Lazarus, Jesus' personal friend, was an example of an adult in need of the life-giving power of Jesus. In the story of Lazarus, described in John 11, the marks of death were advanced and evident, he had been dead and buried for four days. Jesus shouted to Lazarus to bring him to life—but come to life Lazarus did. And so will many adults, who have the privilege of hearing the life-giving message of hope in Jesus Christ.

All of us who know Jesus Christ in a personal way have come to him at some point in time, relinquished our rights to ourselves, given him our lives and called on him to be our Lord. In response, he has put us in an amazing position; Ephesians 2:6 says, "For He raised us from the dead along with Christ and we are seated with Him in the heavenly realms—all because we are one with Christ Jesus."

That's our actual "position" right now, as believers in Jesus. But sometimes our "practice" does not match that spiritual "location" where we sit.

That's what Romans 6–8 and many passages in the book of Galatians are all about. There are also numerous examples in the New Testament and in the Old, in which believers, still very much alive in spiritual reality, grew confused, and complacent, and fell back into some old habits, old insecurities, old misconceptions, old influences that obstructed the full enjoyment and expression of the life within them.

At what point do we begin to fail to live fully alive? Perhaps we were not focusing on Jesus. Perhaps we were functioning in spiritual cruise-control or autopilot, rather than paying attention to our growth and service that a life in Jesus Christ deserves.

We live in a world of the "downward pull." If we do not do our part to keep *any* relationship, human or divine, vibrant and growing, it can easily begin to "slide" at our end.

The Spiritually Alive Person

We know better than to just lie on the couch and wait for food to fall into our mouth. We cannot sit immobile and expect our muscle tone to increase. As believers, who once were dead and now are very much alive, we need to enjoy the vibrant life that a living person has been given. So, what is a spiritually alive person like?

She is glad to be alive. For a true believer, life is a celebration, an act of worship and thanksgiving, even in the hard times that inevitably come during daily real life. "In everything give thanks, for this is the will of God in Christ Jesus" (1 Thessalonians 5:18 NKJV).

She has spiritual activity. She exerts God-provided energy, determination, strength and power to accomplish significant things for the glory of God, the benefit of others, and for personal satisfaction.

She has needs, but they are different from those of a spiritually dead person, who needs only life. Even when we come to Jesus Christ, we still function in the physical realm, where needs continue to abound. We always need to grow as believers in our faith, our conduct, our commitment, and our service, but we know that our *source*, our fulfillment of every need is the source of our life itself, Jesus Christ. He is our "Jehovah Jireh," the Lord, our Provider.

She reproduces life in others. What we are excited about we want to share with others. As "satisfied customers," it is obvious that we want those around us to experience the life we've found, and even when it is deemed politically incorrect to "impose" our faith on others, we understand that to keep hidden the secret to abundant and eternal life would be the height of callous unconcern for the souls of precious people who need God's grace as much as we do.

She has a bright future. Because of the indescribable love and generosity of Jesus Christ, our permanent home is the wondrous and unfathomable beauty of Heaven. For those precious friends who have never met Jesus Christ, there awaits a future as well; an indescribable continuation of eternal death which has already begun for them.

God Asks Women to Live

If we are truly spiritually alive, and in that position of hope and grace forever, what do we need to do to live that way *now*? In the battle to live "life" in a practical way, our greatest enemy is another four-letter word: *Self,* the very "self" that is supposed to be dead.

There was once a little boy whose much loved pet cat had died. He had tremendous difficulty coping with the reality that his feline friend was no longer alive. In fact, the boy was so attached to his pet that he continued to keep the deceased cat in his room until his mother said, in no uncertain terms, that it must be taken to the backyard and buried. After the burial "ceremony," the little boy continued to engage in behavior that his mother found puzzling. Everyday after school, he would hurriedly go to the backyard and come back red-faced and somber. Finally, the concerned mom had to find out why and secretly followed her son to the backyard. She observed that her little boy had buried his pet completely except for the tail, which could be seen sticking out of the dirt. He pulled the cat up out of the dirt by the tail, as he had apparently done numerous times before, and boo-hooed and sobbed about the loss of his pet. He simply couldn't let go of what had been so near and dear to him.

If we're honest, we often act much like that little boy, bereaved over the demise of someone so precious to us—ourselves! It's hard to say goodbye to the self we've lived with so long and loved so much. The way we handle the very real problem of self-love is addressed many times in the New Testament. We cannot, nor need not, deny that it exists for each of us, no matter how determined, how committed we may be in living our life to the fullest for the glory of

God. None of us has "arrived," not even the apostle Paul. "Not that I have already obtained all this, or have already been made perfect, but I press on to take hold of that for which Christ Jesus took hold of me" (Philippians 3:12).

We all still struggle with the "self" within us. The Bible, in its wonderful, practical manner, provides five "snapshots" for us that help us understand what that struggle to live selflessly means.

Selfless Snapshot One: The Dual Crucifixion

The first snapshot is the picture of the dual crucifixion—Jesus' death and our own. Nothing could be more impossible for us to do than to ignore ourselves and what we want. Someone snaps at me and I snap back. Someone hurts me, offends me, misjudges my motives, opposes my opinion, and I retaliate (or want to).

Self interests, self-consciousness, self-confidence, self-focus—self, self, self. Remember how Paul dealt with his own problem of self? Think about these words. He said he was crucified with Christ, nevertheless, he lived, but not the old Paul, it was Christ living in him. Thus he stayed alive in his earthly body by trusting in the Son of God, who loved him and gave himself for him. (See Galatians 2:20.)

That's the secret to doing what we cannot do. We must allow Jesus Christ to live his life in and through us. Only Jesus can live the Christian life, the life of Christ. We get out of the way. Self decreases and he increases, day by day, circumstance by circumstance. More of him, less of us. Jesus does not just "help" us as we copy him in our pattern of behavior, love, and service. As we obey Jesus he actually lives his life through our body, our mind, our emotions, and our will. Amazing.

If we are now new and different people, and we've looked at what an "alive" person looks like, what are we like when we have truly, practically died to our self?

- We don't have any concern about our own "rights." A person who has died no longer has rights.
- We don't require a lot of personal attention. We are not "high maintenance" people.
- We don't expect affirmation, praise, recognition, and we don't spend time worrying about having our own needs met.
- We don't expect to have our ideas approved and accepted by others. Things don't have to go our way.
- We don't worry or stress about *anything*.
- We don't think about ourselves *at all*.

Whew, tall order. Only Jesus lived like that. Only Jesus in us can. When we catch ourselves (and we need to take inventory often) acting, reacting and even thinking like the "old self," we need to remind ourselves to "consider" (as Paul aptly said) that the person-from-the-past is *dead*. Deceased. Passed away forever.

Selfless Snapshot Two: The Living Garden

The second snapshot is the important concept of spiritual life and death as displayed in the picture Jesus showed us of the living garden.

In John 12:24, Jesus talks about seeds that are planted into the ground as "dead" and then "come alive" to produce a great harvest. "Except a corn of wheat fall into the ground and die, it abides alone, but if it dies, it brings forth much fruit" (KJV). His prophetic words were clearly foretelling his own death, but also explaining the principle that our lives reach their full potential when we die to ourselves and come alive in him.

Jesus often used pictures from the world of horticulture. He demonstrated eternal principles through the natural realm of dirt, gardens, fruit trees, planters and harvesters, vines and their branches. In one beautiful gardening illustration, Jesus helps us understand the principle that his life is flowing productively through us as he described the way a vine and its branches coexist and interact. When his life and his love flow through us, like life-infusing minerals and water flow from a vine to its branches, the end result is productive fruitfulness.

Fruit grows directly from the branches, but never without the life of the vine. Jesus is the Vine, we are his branches. John 15:4 says, "Remain in me, and I will remain in you. For a branch cannot produce fruit if it is severed from the vine, and you cannot be fruitful apart from me."

Unless we are connected to the vine, we're just an old, dead stick. A lifeless, helpless stick disconnected from the source of power, energy, and productivity; absolutely unable to do anything of value. No matter how hard we try, how "real" and alive we appear to others, we're still dead.

Selfless Snapshot Three: The Living Sacrifice

Paul admonishes us to "present your bodies a living sacrifice, holy, acceptable unto God, which is your reasonable service" (Romans 12:1 KJV). "Living" and "sacrifice" sound contradictory. Living means life, sacrifice means death. What does this oxymoron mean?

Many paradoxes exist in our divinely inspired Scripture. The Bible tells us to offer our lives to God to bring about the death of the "old us," so that Christ can make a new "us," empowered by his supernatural life. Our weakness and our inadequacy, is exchanged for his strength and his all-sufficiency. How awesome!

Perhaps I'm preoccupied with everyday concerns and all shook up because the store is out of my favorite brand, the service is too slow and the server is "inept," I feel taken for granted and unappreciated, or I got passed over for a promotion. I need to notice that I have taken myself off the altar of personal sacrifice. I am forgetting to seek first the kingdom of God and his righteousness, and not the kingdom of self. How many things are we stressed about that will not matter a hundred years from now? Romans 12:1 says that being a living sacrifice is our reasonable response to all that Jesus has done for us.

When I present my body as a living sacrifice to God, that means I give him all that I am:

- All my rights.
- My reputation, or loss of it, because my commitment is to him and his Word.
- All my desires and future plans. I may never have the money nor the recognition I want to enjoy. My efforts may never be recognized, appreciated, or acknowledged except by him.
- All my time, lived for him. No days off.
- All my possessions—always available for him to use or take away. He has the right to direct our spending, saving, giving. It's all his.
- All my relationships or lack of them.
- My employment, my successes and failures, my hiring and my termination.
- All of myself—my emotions, my health, my thoughts and my activities—my past, present, future. Everything.

Perhaps your mental picture of total "sacrifice" involves a one-time, life-changing, church-camp, sickbed, revival-meeting experience in which you lay yourself down on a spiritual altar. We picture that commitment like putting a thousand dollar bill in the offering plate, "There, that's done." When asked about the time of greatest spiritual impact on our lives, we recall that moment in time over and over, often proudly, and not at all in the spirit Jesus intended, or we might never mention it at all.

Those life-impacting moments are important, but it is interesting that from that point of commitment on, our being a "living sacrifice" actually plays out in twenty-five cent or fifty-cent increments. For instance:

- A friend calls and needs to talk when we're too tired to even think. Relative cost to us: 50¢.

- Our child wants to play a game for the twentieth time in a row. Relative cost to us: 10¢.

- Our husband is feeling romantic and we are definitely not. Cost: $1.

- Our boss failed to plan well and it makes us look bad, again. Cost: 75¢.

- We don't get to express our opinion and wanted to. Cost: 15¢.

- We worked so hard on a ladies' event, but our name is never acknowledged or mentioned. Cost: 50¢.

- Our birthday is forgotten by someone whose special day we always remember. Cost: 25¢.

- We give money to someone in need whose name we don't even know and no one else knows about our sacrifice. Cost: $1.

- Our husband won't admit his mistake and continues to see us at fault. Cost: $1.50.

On and on it goes. Ten cents here, a quarter there, day in and day out. A living sacrifice; wholly acceptable to God, our reasonable service.

Selfless Snapshot Four: Surrender

The white flag of surrender is a military action indicating a complete yielding to the will of a ruler or victorious conqueror. In the era in which Jesus lived, the people were under the oppressive rule of the Roman Empire. The Jews of that day would gladly have surrendered to any conqueror who could free them from Rome and give them back self-rule. But to yield completely to a spiritual liberator? The people struggled with that one, and still do.

In Jesus' day, as in ours, people did not understand that surrendering to Jesus was not a painful defeat. Surrender to Jesus Christ is, in reality, a victory cry. We align ourselves with our conquering hero who will fill our life with all that is good, satisfying, and significant.

People like Abraham had to surrender to God's lordship without knowing his plan, the map, the itinerary, or the details. God gave Abraham a promise to hold on to, and then called him to surrender everything. He told him to leave his country, his people, his father's household and go to a faraway land that God would show him as he went.

What must Abraham have thought? "Does God really expect us to leave behind our friends and relationships? What's my wife going to say? What about food, shelter from the weather, and predators? What about the herds? Will there be enough food for them along the way? Will the soil be fertile? Are we going to like it wherever we're going? I'd really like to hear Plan B, Lord!"

But Abraham followed God because of 1) who God is, and 2) what God promised. That God is the same God today. All of us are called to leave our past behind and follow God's promises for our lives.

Some Christians, such as missionaries called to foreign fields, emulate Abraham a little more dramatically. They learn a new culture and language, downsize their living standard, leave the security of home, and say goodbye to family and friends for an unknown length of time. But in Genesis 15:1, God says, "Do not be afraid, Abram. I *am* your shield; your exceedingly great reward" (emphasis mine, NKJV). In God and his promises, we have all we need to counter our fears so we can serve him. Jesus Christ offers us a "blank contract" to sign for life and eternity. After we add our spiritual signature of commitment to the document, he fills in the blanks as he sees fit, which is only right since he is God. He is love. He is sovereign, and absolutely trustworthy. He cannot and will not, ever fail us. Letting him lead is all about trusting him.

Sometimes we let our attitudes, our misconceptions and misunderstandings get in the way of our total surrender to Jesus Christ. Fear sometimes gets in our way.

Perhaps you thought life's journey would be with a loving spouse, and that's not the path you've been on, and may never be. Perhaps you pictured a houseful of chattering children, but God's journey with you has not been down that road. Some have experienced perpetual job security and a great career, but your husband lost his job, or you lost yours. How can we surrender when we don't know what we're surrendering to? The road might get real bumpy, and we'd like to avoid that route, if at all possible. But like Abraham, we do know who we're surrendering to. We're surrendering to God and we can absolutely trust him. Remember Jeremiah 29:11? The Lord looks us straight in the eye and promises: "For I know the plans I have for you. They are plans for good and not for disaster—to give you a future and a hope." And note this: His plans for you are carefully designed and customized with an eternal purpose, not just randomly thrown together.

My most intense desire for my children was that they would grow up to love and serve Jesus Christ with all their hearts, for all their lives. However, attached to that constant prayer was a haunting element of fear. Because my husband was involved in ministry and our lives were so intertwined with his calling, I knew that Satan's passionate counter-desire was to destroy my children and their faith.

God graciously led me to his promises in Scripture that I held on to like a lifeline in stormy seas. They came to me from the Lord at just the right moments, and they were absolute fact in the midst of uncertainty; they proved to be true, as all of God's promises do. I learned through relinquishing my own fears, worries, and dreams that the secret to peace and confidence lies in our willingness to trust in Jesus alone and to hold tightly to that "evidence unseen" in his personalized promises to us.

Surrender is not optional. It's absolutely essential.

Selfless Snapshot Five: The Free Slave

The last "snapshot" in Scripture that helps us see how to live through this "death to self" is the picture of the free slave.

The twenty-first chapter of Exodus includes a long list of requirements concerning Hebrew servants. One of the most interesting
commands appears in verses 2 and 5–6.

> If you buy a Hebrew slave, he is to serve for only six years. Set him
> free in the seventh year and he will owe you nothing for his freedom
> . . . But the slave may plainly declare, "I love my master, my wife, and
> my children. I would rather not go free." If he does this, his master
> must present him before God. Then his master must take him to the
> door and publicly pierce his ear with an awl. After that, the slave will
> belong to his master forever.
>
> (Exodus 21:2, 5–6)

This idea of voluntary servitude, the option being offered to the
Hebrew people, is foreign to us. The concept of slavery is abhorrent
to our culture, and rightly so. One person enslaving another person,
both created by God, is horrible, but the biblical imagery regarding
slavery is a metaphor for what it means to be a willing bondservant of
Jesus Christ. Yes, it is a paradox that at the same time a person can be
a slave and be truly free, but it captures how a child of God chooses
to willingly place her life, future, and destiny into the hands of the
sovereign, divine Lord of all. In doing this the surrendered person
relinquishes her rights to own herself from that day forward. Jesus
truly becomes Lord of all; Lord of everything.

Does that sound like the compartmentalized concept of "faith" and
"religion" that is espoused by much of contemporary society? Does a
slave of Jesus Christ add "church" to their life simply as a routine and
only when it is convenient? Can a servant consider herself belonging
totally to Jesus Christ, while living however she wants when it comes
to practical life in the real world?

David was a king, a person of undeniable importance. His was
a household name; his status was far above that of a sports hero
or "American Idol" winner. In spite of his political stature, David
understood the concept of willing servitude as he wrote the words

in Psalm 40 verses 6 and 8: "Sacrifice and offering you did not desire, but my ears you have *pierced* ... 'I desire to do your will, O my God'" (NIV).

David was saying that he wanted God's leadership. In addition, if we examine the cross-reference for Psalm 40:6, we find ourselves arriving at the passage we just read in Exodus 21. David may also be saying that he was God's "slave" by choice, in the same way that Hebrew slaves had their ears pierced to show that they were offering themselves in life-long service to their master.

In the New Testament, the word used to describe Jesus and his followers as servants of God is *doulos*, the very lowliest kind of slavery possible, an indentured state in which the slave's rights simply do not exist and the master is absolute lord of everything, including life and death. In beautiful expressions of willing surrender to the Lordship of Jesus Christ, Paul, Peter, James, and Jude all describe themselves in scripture as *doulos*. Bill Bright, the founder and life-long leader of Campus Crusade for Christ, only wanted his funeral epitaph to read, "A slave of Jesus Christ."

We were all born in slavery to sin, with no way, no help, and no hope to change our desperate condition. The sentence of death was upon us. We were absolutely helpless as slaves to do anything to free ourselves. We were *doulos* and he was King and Master of the universe; we were a royal "mismatch." But Jesus, in a horrendously painful choice, exchanged his freedom for our enslavement, and took into his own body the pain, death, and hell this divine transaction required. Now, in God's great grace, we have been elevated to the blessed position of children of God, his precious jewels, and joint heirs with Jesus Christ.

So now we choose, by our will, to give him the absolute surrender of ourselves that he deserves. We are free slaves.

In the 1924 Olympics in Paris, a young Scottish athlete became known for his determination to do things God's way, regardless of the personal cost. Eric Liddell made a decision that many found unthinkable and irrational: to drop out of the racing event at which he excelled, the 100-yard dash, because the qualifying races were being held on a Sunday. As his competitors were participating in the heats, Liddell was preaching to a small congregation of believers near the racetrack.

Because of his commitment to a higher calling, Liddell instead entered another race, the 400-yard dash, a race for which he had not trained and felt ill equipped to run. However, with God as his source of strength and endurance, he ran the race, finished five yards ahead of his closest competitor, and set a new world record.

Yet his gold medal was far from Eric Liddell's greatest achievements. After Paris, Liddell ran the great race for Jesus Christ as a missionary to China, where he had been raised as a child. In 1943, he was imprisoned by the Japanese military in a concentration camp; there he served faithfully as the Lord's servant to the other prisoners. While expressing his love for Jesus through service to others within the camp, Liddell suffered a brain tumor that left him partially paralyzed and physically debilitated. Liddell's last words were expressed from his hospital bed on February 21, 1945, as he quietly shared with his nurse, Annie, his secret to such an extraordinarily committed life. "Annie, it's complete surrender," he whispered.

Let's be honest enough now to let the spotlight shine on us, to sit under the interrogation lamp. Since it's just you, me, and God here together, and nobody else is able to listen to our thoughts or to perform a spiritual echocardiogram on our heart of hearts, do we honestly think that what God asks of us is just too hard, too demanding of our time, energy, and selflessness? Do we find it plausible that in order to make the gospel a little more palatable in today's PC and free-thinking culture that the Lord may have watered down his standards and requirements for his people a bit? Does God desire to recruit more servants from today's secular "people pool" by offering them fewer expectations and demands in exchange for a comfortable people-friendly faith?

184

Think seriously about Isaac Watts words: "Must I be carried through the skies on flowery beds of ease, while others fought to win the prize and sailed through bloody seas?"[11] Must I? That's heavy. That's hard.

Old expectations: Ease, comfort, sunny days and moonlit nights. Easy answers. Quick solutions. Comfortable hammocks, fresh breezes, mild winters, temperate summers. Green lights, short lists, fun and games. *My* way.

New Reality: Question marks. Struggles. Painful stings, deep-down aches, and long waits. Cavernous cliffs and narrow, winding paths. Crashing descents. Upward climbs. Rocky roads and no U-turns. *His* way.

God's resources and new expectations: Challenges . . . solutions. Failure . . . success. Long waits . . . perfect timing. Free falling . . . safety net. Downs . . . up. Blind curves . . . broad, lighted highway. Dead end . . . wide open gate to golden streets. Complete surrender . . . total victory! *His* way—*mine*.

What does the big picture of life as a believer in Jesus Christ really look like? We've seen glimpses of the good, the bad, and the ugly. What can we actually expect to encounter? Demanding tasks and intolerant people, sometimes the one in our own mirror. Failures and successes. Red lights and green lights. Following the leader, or feeling the presence of people behind us, walking in our tracks. Our willing demise of our own self and the life and eternity-changing discovery that in *losing* life, we truly *find* it. How can we face what we must? What shall we do when things asked of us along the journey are difficult?

The key is our single focus on the person of Jesus Christ, the Author and Finisher of it all. He is the divine title page all the way to the eternal index. He is our guide from spiritual birth to the awesome splendor of everlasting life. He has all the resources we will ever require, to be and do all we must, already purchased with his own life.

185

The tolerance we need to deal correctly with irregular people has as its source the same precious grace that God extended toward us as an indescribable gift. The same Lord is the generous provider of the patience to wait, and the courage and wisdom to proceed when the time is right. Jesus will enable us to release our grasp on what we should hold onto lightly or not at all, and provide the strength and endurance to hold onto what deserves to be grasped tightly. He will be the Leader that we follow, and the Equipper and Enabler in every leadership initiative we are called upon to take.

Jesus Christ, our earthly and eternal focus; the one who both escorts and welcomes us into his indescribable presence for ever and ever and ever, Amen. And nothing again will ever be hard.

> I place my life in the hands of God.
> Those hands so scarred, now outstretched for me.
> Wherever it may be, over land . . . over sea . . .
> May Thy will sublime, O Thou God divine,
> Be mine.[12]

Chapter 7 Study Questions

1. **When you came to Christ for salvation,** what was the most dramatic, noticeable transformation that you, and maybe other people, observed in your life? What spiritual changes took place that no one else may have seen, but the Bible says took place just as certainly as if they had been visible?

2. ***Since you came to Jesus for forgiveness and life,*** what elements of "self" have you continued to struggle with from time to time, or often? Where are your "Achilles heels," areas of vulnerability and weakness that you feel keep you from being as effective and available to God as you want to be? Are you willing to surrender those fortified "kingdoms" that continue to be controlled by yourself to the complete oversight of the Lord Jesus Christ?

3. **Ask Jesus to make you aware** of each incident and moment in time in which you are dominated by your old "self," and immediately let the Lord take charge of everything you are: What you say, how you think and the ways in which you act and react. Remember that your old self is dead and forever powerless to control you, as you surrender daily, and moment by moment, to the Lord Jesus Christ, who is ready to live his life through you.

4. ***Think of the damaging evidences of your "old self"*** that are no longer a part of your new life. Thank God for each victory, each milestone, each personal triumph, every evidence of the new, victorious life within you. Determine to be the Lord's willing "bondservant" every day of your life until you see him face to face. Ask him for his power and empowerment to do this.

5. If you would like to do a personal study using this chapter's topic, here are some Scriptures you may want to refer to:

Genesis 15:1
Exodus 21
Psalm 40:6, 8
Matthew 10:38
Mark 8
Mark 5:21–43
Luke 7:11–17
Luke 14
John 3:16–18
John 10:10
Romans 3:23
Romans 5:15–19
Romans 7:24
Romans 6:5, 6–11
Romans 6:4–14
Romans 7–8
Romans 12:1
I Corinthians 15:21
Galatians 2:20
Galatians 3
Galatians 5:22–24
Ephesians 2:1–10
Philippians 2:7

Notes

1. Aaron Senseman and Cliff Young, "Before There Was Time," Caedmon's Call, *In the Company of Angels-A Call to Worship*, MMI Essential Records compact disk B00005NNK8, 2001.

2. Helen H. Lemmel, "Turn Your Eyes Upon Jesus," 1922.

3. Gloria Gaither and William J. Gaither, "Something Beautiful," 1971.

4. Jann Mitchell, *A Little Girls Dream,* ed. Alice Gray and Barbara Baumgardner, *Stories for the Heart: The Third Collection*, (Sisters, Oregon: Multnomah Publishers, 2000), 155.

5. Billy Rose, *If We Had Hurried*, ed. Alice Gray, *Stories for the Heart: The Original Collection*, (Sisters, Oregon: Multnomah Publishers, 1996), 213.

6. Dick Baker, "His Way, Mine," *Keep Looking Up*, Word Records, 1958.

7. Philip Yancey, *What's So Amazing About Grace*, (Grand Rapids, MI: Zondervan, 1997).

8. Aaron Senseman, "God Who Saves," Caedmon's Call, *In the Company of Angels-A Call to Worship*, MMI Essential Records, compact disk B00005NNK82001, 2001.

9. *The Artist,* author unknown, ed. Alice Gray, *Stories for the Heart: The Second Collection*, (Sisters, Oregon: Multnomah Publishers, 2000), 294.

10. Mary Gardiner Brainard, 1837–1905, "Not Knowing."

11. Isaac Watts, "Am I a Soldier of the Cross?," 1709.

12. Dick Baker, "His Way, Mine," *Keep Looking Up*, Word Records, 1958.

Kathie Reimer

Kathie Reimer is an author, educator, encourager, and friend to many in the ministry community and beyond. Her love for children and studied spiritual depth combine to make her a leading authority on teaching children to love God from the earliest of ages. As a pastor's wife for over 30 years, Kathie has had the opportunity to teach the Bible to women across the country and has had a strong influence on them in their walk with the Lord. Kathie has authored a series of three books on parenting: *1001 Ways to Introduce Your Child to God, 1001 Ways to Help Your Child Walk With God* and *1001 Ways to Introduce Your Child to the Bible*. She has three grown children and five grandchildren. She and her husband, Jim, reside in Charlotte, NC.

Lisa Whittle

With a heart and passion for ministry, Lisa Whittle is a unique motivator with a desire to reach women and point them to Christ. Born into the family of a pastor, Lisa felt an early personal call to ministry, leading her to become the visionary implementer of various women's events, including the **Breath of Heaven Conferences for Women**. A graduate of Liberty University, Lisa has done masters work in Marriage and Family Counseling and has had her writing featured in HomeLife Magazine. Co-founder of the organization, *Real Influence*, Lisa and her husband Scott reside just outside of Charlotte, N.C., with their three young children.